Footbridge Above
the Falls

Footbridge Above the Falls

Poems by Forty-Eight Northwest Poets

Edited by

David D. Horowitz

Rose Alley Press
Seattle, Washington

Published in the United States of America by Rose Alley Press

For information, please contact the publisher:

Rose Alley Press
David D. Horowitz, President
4203 Brooklyn Avenue NE, #103A
Seattle, WA 98105-5911
Telephone: 206-633-2725
Email: rosealleypress@juno.com
Website: www.rosealleypress.com

ISBN: 978-0-9906812-2-9

Cover photograph of Multnomah Falls in Oregon: "Columbia River Gorge, OR, in the Fall of 2016" by Murali Narayanan, https://muralipix.com/2017/05/06/columbia-river-gorge-or-in-the-fall-of-2016/. Rose Alley Press thanks Murali for his kindness and generosity. To see more of his photography, visit "Murali Narayanan Photography: Travel Blog with emphasis on Nature Photography" at https://muralipix.com.

Printed in the United States of America

CONTENTS

EDITOR'S NOTE

Welcome to *Footbridge Above the Falls*, the third Rose Alley Press poetry anthology. This anthology, like its two predecessors, features work by poets of diverse background and aesthetic inclination. I hope it finds an equally diverse readership.

That said, *Footbridge Above the Falls*, also like its predecessors, pays respectful attention to poetic pattern—particularly rhyme and meter. Pacific Northwest poets are not especially known for their commitment to rhyme, meter, and form, yet some of the United States's finest formal poets live here. I love poetry of all kinds and am grateful for every poem in this anthology, formal or not. I am glad, though, to highlight the work of poets who write in form—whether often or occasionally, traditionally or experimentally. Stereotypes blind us to complex realities, such as the Pacific Northwest being home to a remarkable range of poets who write in rhyme, meter, and form. Their work needs to be better known. There is no official "Northwest" aesthetic, and those who do not write like a perceived majority nevertheless merit an attentive readership. *Footbridge Above the Falls* attempts to help poets find that readership, and if you are reading this now: thank you.

Now, I am not a novice to literary endeavor, and I have heard and engaged in my share of debates about contemporary American poetry. I unapologetically love and promote rhymed metrical verse—but never in the spirit of a culture war. Dogma and its hate-filled offspring too often dominate political arenas; they needn't silence, discourage, or denigrate anyone because of dissenting aesthetic commitments. So, poems of all sorts populate this book. This is a sharing, a meeting-place for mutual appreciation, a haven for the open-minded weary of expectation they join enclaves to prove the mettle of petty, monitored loyalty. Here are some fine poems; read them, share them, debate their meaning and worth—and then reread them and reread them. This book is about the poems in it. Feel however you feel about them; I only hope you read and consider them. And don't worry if you begin to feel your perspective shift or broaden; that's only poetry doing its good work. Indeed, such broadening is one primary reason tyrants so deeply fear poetry and writers generally; writers inspire the imagination, and a free imagination will not be a slave.

So, now, this book is filled with poems waiting for you. If you're ready, then, for a literary adventure, start reading—and, yes, rereading is encouraged, too.

David D. Horowitz
Editor and Publisher, Rose Alley Press

Footbridge Above
the Falls

Richard Wakefield

BROUGHT TO LIGHT

The wind tore through on trash-collection day
and scattered secrets up and down the street.
Our private lives lie jumbled, indiscreet,
though what belonged to whom is hard to say.
An upwind neighbor's Playboy Playmates pose
in Mrs. Jones's begonias, broken loose.
Losing lotto tickets deck a spruce
like anemic leaves where disappointment grows.
Intimate prescriptions and bills past-due
bear names, though none the finder recognizes.
And what if he did? The catalog of vices
shows us almost nothing unique or new.
What's strange is our capacity for shame
when what we strive to hide is all the same.

RHETORIC

His middle-class suburban house and yard
and her blue-collar rental townhouse past
were far apart, but love has scant regard
for trivialities of social caste.

One day "we *pluribus unum*, babe," he joked.
She didn't get it. He explained. She smiled
but didn't laugh. The awkward exchange provoked
a standoff. But love is love. They reconciled.

In private he thought the way she spoke was quaint,
and it wasn't as if he didn't know what she meant.
In public, though, he drew the line at "ain't"
and double negatives and "should have went."

His public "she and I" for "me and her"
were fine, but when they were alone he said
not "who" but "whom." What was sillier
than hoity-toity talk like that in bed?

At last with "snob" and "hick" their dissonance
confirmed it takes more kinds of intercourse
than one to keep a story-book romance
from ending in a grammar-book divorce.

TWO ARTISTS

— after The Gross Clinic *by Thomas Eakins*
(surgery: from the Greek for *work* and *hand)*

The scalpel, wound, and pencil glimmer bright
with lurid red that draws the viewer's gaze
across a flat expanse of somber grays.
Eakins puts himself to Gross's right,
making the artist and surgeon counterparts.
Their hands display the same precision grip
to yield their implements, the scalpel tip
and pencil point engaged in equal arts.

Between them, her hands distorted into claws,
a woman throws her arm across her eyes—
the patient's mother. She personifies
the fragile human anguish Eakins draws
but Gross cannot allow himself to see,
a sense too deep to probe with surgery.

LOTTERY

He calls me when he's had too much to drink
at three a.m. Behind his voice I hear
a bottle kiss a glass with a stuttering clink.
He likes to talk about our junior year.
He talks of far more girls than I recall,
more staggering home at dawn, more missing class.
I nod. It was the 'sixties, after all;
I let the most unlikely stories pass.
We didn't see it then, the great divide
ahead, but who at twenty-one foresees
how whimsically the gods or fates decide
the twisting courses of our histories?
My number wasn't called. His was. His war,
my college took us down divergent streams.
He calls my number when he's grasping for
the strength to swim against his troubled dreams.
And so our one-way conversation goes,
these half-invented fantasies of his,
across the years and miles, as if to close
the gap between what might have been and is.

Richard Wakefield

A HOLDOUT

The farm held out against the sprawl
the modern age embraced,
until its fencelines faced
three subdivisions and a mall.

At last death left the farm unmanned,
the fields untilled, until
the heirs could break the will
and reap a fortune from the land.

While they worked deals the land grew dense
with alder, running vines,
and even seedling pines
behind the sagging wire fence.

Thus unproductive nature bloomed
perversely, for a time,
then yielded to prime
suburban lots, so smoothly groomed.

It's no use asking whether deep
in us there's such a place,
or if we've purged all trace
of what we can't afford to keep.

THE CROW WHO SAID "HELLO"

This morning on my walk I heard a crow
beside a brackish puddle rasp "Hello."
The water in the pre-dawn dark was black
as he, but he saw something gazing back,
just as Narcissus did. He cocked his head,
he preened and gazed, "Hello, hello," he said.
There was no marble bust, no chamber door,
and nothing as profound as *Nevermore*,
just "Hello!" He grated out the word,
then flew away like any speechless bird.
Had I imagined what I heard and saw?
But how could I mistake a raucous caw
coughed up from such an ordinary crow
to sound like that articulate "hello"?
It undermines a person's confidence
when what we sense conflicts with what makes sense.

WILLFUL MISREADING

A nurse log, rotted almost down to duff,
gave rise to Douglas fir in ragged rank,
as if some hand had set a fence of rough-
hewn posts along this rocky, root-bound bank.
By braided years the river shifts its course
according to unseen necessities,
and swollen with the snowmelt turns its force
against the bank to undercut the trees.
Sometimes they topple and are borne away
in one dramatic, cataclysmic crash,
while others angle slowly, day by day,
to kiss their reflections with the merest splash.
These days the scene suggests a metaphor
that takes a willful blindness to ignore.

By WINTER LIGHT

An old man at his kitchen window sees
by winter light, beyond a tumbled stone wall,
now held by weeds and skeletons of trees,
the garden gone untended since the fall.
Hard to see among the mud and moss
and rampant tansy tainted yellow-brown,
a tiny dun-gray bird flits quick across
his narrow view, back and forth, then down
to earth to peck at specks. For all its tries
against its beak it takes so few to eat
the old man marvels that such a meager prize
can stoke the fist-sized spark of vital heat.
It flutters up the thorny hedge and skips
from vine to branch to probe the dark decay.
The old man tries his tongue and teeth and lips
against some words: *sparrow? swallow? jay?*
Once, the words he needed simply came
and bound themselves to creatures, one by one,
but now the bird flies off without a name,
as if some earthly knot has come undone.

CONVERSATION ON THE ROAD

In hooded ponchos, gloves and boots, we look
like paper cut-outs glued to a page of rain.
Still, dry inside and almost warm, we took
this walk, we thought, to straighten out the pain

of legs and hearts. Great Thoughts we thought would come,
taut muscles loosened, stretched . . . just down the trail.
But limited to stiff and clunky moves from
our protective gear, we're really dressed to fail.

Let's take our scissors, cut us from the page.
Free our angular outlines, so flat and stiff,
and open up the insulated rage.
Then, undressed from illusion, we can lift

our language past its baleful norm. If true,
I'd choose to speak in rhyming words to you.

A FAMILY HISTORY

Life went on. We ate with silver, off china plates—
we never grabbed for rolls but used the silver tongs.
And the grand piano played in rhythm to our fates.

Four kids all young, not one of us anticipates
our Father's grief: lost job and everything gone wrong.
Life went on. We ate with silver, off china plates.

We loved his music. Father played the piano straight
till dinner, his long fingers birthing each old song
as the grand piano told the rhythm of his fate.

So when he stopped, it seemed we simply had to wait.
We never thought the break, the silence, would last long.
Life went on. We ate with silver, off china plates.

Giggles and songs—he heard our voices resonate
off the sounding board, and his haunting was prolonged.
He knew the piano held the rhythm of his fate.

One year—we still remember well that final date.
He sat down, hands back at the keys where they belonged.
Life went on. We ate with silver, off china plates,
while the grand piano sang the rhythm of our fates.

PASS IT ON

Today some pocket fuzz finds your fingers
and you roll it into a worry bead.
Even your hands know how worry lingers,
takes shape to resemble anything, leads

to hesitation with each decision.
Now you're so careful at each dark doorway,
know a stumble's a cascade collision.
You could stay inside. (There the sun can't lay

its cancer eggs on your pale freckled face.)
But *Beware!* isn't a greeting. Let it go.
Try using balance as a starting place.
Fear feeds freely on "How am I to know?"

Your dad used duct tape on his pants-seam tear.
Cut cardboard to seal sole holes in his shoes.
Said "It could be worse," didn't seem to care.
But your ears heard a chorus—lots to lose.

Let your daughter wander, just not free-range.
There is still time to loosen worry's hood.
You'll shorten up your shadow, slip some change
and risk, inside the multiples of could.

Patricia Bollin

FRAMEWORK

A woman walks the grassy river shore,
where seeds fall easily from her open hands.
Apostle geese—they follow wanting more,
bob their heads in rhythm as each speck lands.
Is this a masked equation: give/control?
Here she's a jesus to each bird. But then
their hunger grows. Their honking turns quite bold.
She slips to blur. I watch the birds contend
with loss, their stately air of disregard.
If I could practice such a basic style
(a subtle swagger shouldn't be too hard)
perhaps the ache would only last awhile.
But I live in the register of next.
And you have redefined yourself as ex.

AN ATTRACTION TO:

tables set properly,
knives turned cutting edge in,
cloth napkins for each lap;

precise rules, balanced scales,
equations' equal signs,
measuring cups, yardsticks;

dials, hot and cold faucets,
schedules and calendars,
mirrored images, twins;

symmetrical objects,
drawings by engineers,
framed paintings that hang straight;

alphabetical lists,
common words and greetings,
roll of dice when charted;

moon cycles and seasons,
science, earth as a sphere,
planets and their orbits:

set patterns, harmonics,
sense of even footing,
the refuge of order.

WHO TURNED THE EARTH

In a window seat on a train between cities, I dozed.
I rested my head on the glass. It trembled my brain
in a daymare of other's lives. I opened and closed
my eyes on a fogged expanse of brown fields. My train,

like a bored stiff dragon, dragged past hills in the haze.
It seemed out of time till it whisked by a signal or shed.
I missed what human forms we might've passed. In a daze
I fleshed out, as I drifted, some living some dead

who'd carved the furrows, spaded hard dirt to post fences,
hauled seed down the potholed gravel roads, nursed
the smudge pots nights in smoke against frost. My senses
never had gathered who turned the earth. I'd cursed

those wrongheaded voters far from the hives of my towers.
I shuttled through dreams of the land, a few drowsy hours.

THE WIRE SAID

"... we have been most ourselves, when we have opened our doors..."
— *Amy Davidson, in* The New Yorker

Held up behind a red in evening rain,
my FM station on, I heard a man
who'd left his house in rubble, crossed a plain
and then a sea, gone north without a plan,
now faced a razor wire fence—it met
horizon at both ends. The wire said
a vast estate of folk more fortunate
had spread this far, and that its forbears bled
a sea to claim it. Then a rush of surf
it seemed poured through the radio—a gust
blown here, I thought, across the bordered turf,
from where the nomad shifted in the dust.
His ragged English rode like froth on flood.
It floated through the wire, blood to blood.

NOMAD'S HOUSE

I'd seen the black wooden chair. Ikea, I'd guessed,
intact but akilter out back of the Thai place. They kept
the slatty thing there, for someone, a cook say, to rest
on his breaks. Last winter dawn, a bearded man slept

a bit tilted on it, zipped in brown jacket with black
wool cap, stained gray pants, and paint-splattered boots.
Arms round his chest and perched-owl still, with his back
to the wall, he posed for a news clip no one would shoot.

I stepped light as I could past that broadcast on loss,
my trespass, I hoped, no disturbance, this alley his home
for the night at least, the parking slots I walked across
his uncluttered parlor under its airy dark dome.

I'm stirred, how, in the open and cold, he slept,
head erect in the little lot where his life had been swept.

FAMILY GATHERING

The streets will teem with swells of witness again,
the crowd's magnitude risen to match the crime.
Batons held overhead by those helmeted men
in ballistic Kevlar vests, it will be time,

and soon enough the guard's hard line will advance,
the thousands packed close in protest pressed, pressed back
against walls and fences, the near-breathless congregants
prodded, incensed, panicked—then, the attack,

the bludgeons swung down in quick arcs to crack skulls
and clavicles, as if, this time, that would quiet
the storm, as if such crackdown ever dulls
outrage. But once again, they'll try it—

young uniformed men with clubs blood-crown their kin.
They'll do it for their king's blind eye and cold grin.

AFTER COFFEE

— for Christian Wiman

I shuffled, really, living room to bed.
No one saw me. You can take my word.
En route I mumbled. Who knows what I said.
But I can tell you, it occurred.

It was likely something I just wondered.
A question that reopened its own case.
It wasn't whispered, and it wasn't thundered.
A query broadcast into space.

And recumbent, there I shifted, late.
I think the coffee wanted me to think.
But the trouble's in the bones, innate.
I guess the soul's afraid to sink.

As if it, like the body, had a weight.
And aging's inching out on thinner ice.
And there's no more beyond that certain date.
So with each step one best think twice.

Eventually I slept, without an answer.
The mattress must have settled me somehow.
But with all our drownings, strokes, and cancer. . . .
Well, you and I touch now.

HERE AND GONE

So you went missing, disappeared inside,
like water into water, cloud in cloud.
You were still here. It wasn't like you'd died.

Warm to the touch, your flesh occupied,
you were here as ever, and I was proud.
But you'd gone missing, disappeared inside,

pretending presence. Though you hadn't lied.
Isn't some inwardness to be allowed?
You lived here. It wasn't like you'd died.

Your scent and breath so good to lie beside
those years of nights, those years we plowed.
No you weren't missing, disappeared. Inside

you somewhere hid a child I knew who cried,
who went unheard by all the harried crowd
but was still here. It wasn't like you'd died.

I sought you out down in your dark. I tried.
I wound up thrashing, tangled in your shroud,
and missed you as you disappeared inside.
Still here, it was a little like you'd died.

COVER

We have our practiced ways to come and go.
I let the screen door swing back on its hinges,
bang the jamb behind me, and you know
I'm out for now. You pull your micro-binges,
chew on heels of baguette you won't swallow—
yes, your private business, but I've guessed.
Your hurt's like mine—not so hard to follow.
There's your port, my scotch, on one oak chest.

My comeback's quiet, crawling into bed
long after your last page. My wrist will graze
your shoulder, say I'm here with nothing said.
You're bolder—over breakfast, words ablaze.
No matter—either way provides good cover.
No pitching through the dark inside one's lover.

THAT ERA'S AIR

It's possible in the open air to smother.
The atmosphere of what's called love can choke,
and maybe no one saves you from the other.

It happened on our lawn. My baby brother
got lost in the plot before he spoke.
It's possible, in hope-filled air, to smother.

He needed care, and there she was, our mother.
He'd splash the little blow-up pool, she'd smoke,
and no one dared to save one from the other.

Not I, not Grandma, and where was our father?
Dad showed his care by marrying his work.
It's plausible, no? That era's air could smother

any kid, right under normal's cover.
And so it did. The tale is not baroque.
Maybe no one saves one from another.

Now Mom's gone, and he's a man, that toddler
in the plastic pond. Or does he soak,
still docile in the lilac'd air, and smother?
Maybe no love saves us from each other.

Jed Myers

DROWNING

This new solitude, just when summer's come on,
and with it more cold, a steady surprise of rain—
each morning, I grasp it again, you've gone

back to your walk-up loft, the daybed, withdrawn
to the old knowns, your tea strong, your yogurt plain,
and your solitude renewed. Summer's come on

like a strange monsoon—in blows oblivion,
erasing horizon. I scan the near terrain
each morning, and grasp it again, you're gone.

The still and quiet here in the dark before dawn
prove not a thing a busy dream can't explain.
But this new solitude, just when summer's come on,

and here I thought we'd bathe our joys in the sun—
this waking alone soaks in like a stone-gray stain.
Each morning, I gasp on it again. We're done.

I want to climb through the window, onto the lawn,
fall to my knees on the wet grass, call through the rain . . .
but in this new solitude summer's brought on
this morning, I grasp it—for you, I'm gone.

BIG DADDY'S LAMENT FOR BIG MOMMA

"There are times—times, boy—when I dream of death.
Time is a dream, now, of her face in the rain.
These times, boy, I feel I have nothing left.

Time centers around the way that she left
yet time has no way to center this pain.
There are times—times, boy—when I dream of death.

My time is a weight, a burden, a heft
to carry another day—then again—then again.
These times, boy, I feel I have nothing left.

Time saved me from the swinging—those roots—that cliff,
yet her branches still bleed now, still bleed in my brain.
There are times—times, boy—when I dream of death.

Time calls it passage? Boy, I call it theft.
In my dreams, the tile is a burning red plain.
In these times, boy, I feel I have nothing left.

Yet I will keep going—I'll wander—I'll drift
to that last meeting place, and I will walk in.
But there are times—times, boy—when I dream of death.
These times, boy, I feel I have nothing left."

THE GANG HOUSE GARDEN THIEF'S LOVE BALLAD

For your garden, I will find you hot corner petals.
I will put them in my Crown Royal bag.
I will search past the weeds—the thickets—the nettles—
search past the Suckas and their impossible tags
and share with you my world in stems and colors
beyond reds and blues (those handkerchief flags).
I will give you my lavenders beyond the hard metals
in 45s, concrete, and faded doo-rags,
for your love creates me, and love never settles
for environment, so I work. I'll pick them. I'll snag.
For your garden, I will find you hot corner petals.
I will put them in my Crown Royal bag.

SONG FOR MRS. EULALAH

— *after John Dryden's "Song For St. Cecilia's Day"*

"In harmony, heavenly harmony
  in universal love"
                    they cry:
as nature underneath a row
    of preaching deacons lay
(they would not adorn her head).
Church folks' banish is heard on high:
    "Mean old Mrs. McDaniels dead."
And music, in its power to obey
order and stations, makes its leap
        but cannot leave or ground the dread.

What passion cannot music raise and quell.
    Yet sisters break their *concha* shells
as angry deacons stand their ground
in irreverence. Her loved ones' faces fell
    yet the choir comes alive in sound.

The trumpet blows but cannot summon Gabriel.
The mezzo-sopranos sing of Ariel
    yet this hearth is an upraised altar
encamped against her on her side.
Her dying notes are never taken in stride
    yet the beat calls the crowd to a fever.

But, Lord, what can "the one" teach tonight?
What voice can bring now heat or light
    away from her heretical praise?
Apollo's cynicism that masks as sight
cries in its form over her wayward ways
    but cannot disguise itself as love.

Yet the people need power, and there she lays.
The procession moves but not with the spheres
    in her last and dreadful hour.
The church parlor pageant shall devour
    but no bugles are heard on high.
The alive are still with us, the dead have died.
    Yet no music here will retune the sky.

DESCEND

And what of those who have no voice
and no belief, dumbstruck and hurt by love,
no bathysphere to hold them in the depths?
Descend with them and learn and be reborn
to the changing light. We all began without it,
and some were loved and some forgot the love.
Some withered into hate and made a living
hating and rehearsing hate until they died.
The shriveled ones, chatter of the powerful—
they all go on. They go on. You must descend
among the voiceless where you have a voice,
barely a whisper, unheard by most, a wave
among the numberless waves, a weed torn
from the sandy bottom. Here you are. Begin.

BILDUNGSROMAN

— i. m. Seamus Heaney

Because for us all things were living
the night train could not pass unwatched—
the way it threw the forest shadows
spinning across our bedroom wall,
the way it shook the house, the way
the revving diesel blew its top—
so I climbed the metal ladder up
to the upper bunk to see the light
that cast the passing images,
and somehow slipped and stuck my foot
right through the bedroom window glass.
No cut but a shock of the real
and a brother's mockery for trying
to see beyond, and a moment's crying.

HANGMAN

A Big Chief tablet and a Bic
between us on the car's back seat,
the scaffold drawn, and underneath
a code of dashes in a row
for seven letters. Part of a stick-
figure fixed to the noose's O

for every letter missed, until
if I'm not careful my poor guy
will hang with x's for his eyes.
My brother parlays his resource
for big boy words with taunting skill:
"It starts with *d* and rhymes with *force.*"

But I don't know the word, don't know
the wet world being slapped away
by wiper blades, or why the day
moved like an old stop-action film
or an interrupted TV show
about a family on the lam.

I let myself be hanged, and learn
a new word whispered out of fear,
though it will be another year
before I feel the house cut loose,
my dangling body and the burn
of shame enclosing like a noose.

TO HYGEIA

Goddess, I have watched your motions gratify the world.
Votaries of all casts and ages, genders, voices,
bow to you as they must, for nothing follows without you.

I once met a man in an iron lung, puffing his words,
and youth was a much-too-long parade of unfortunate data:
the infirm, the wizened, the washout, the accidental suicide . . .

An old man with a tinkling highball sat like a lord
orating, *When I was a boy*, and we knew a story was coming.
I never minded those times, being an odd duck
who actually listened, but the lesson I failed to get was the one
he always meant: *One of these days, you smug twit,*
you'll be me.

            Now my sage joints prophesy like rats
from a leaking ship, and every morning's gulp of pills
pules in silent offering to Hygeia. *Keep moving*
until you stop. The hell with the good opinion of others.
Wisdom of age, goddess—the sort we laugh about
if lucky enough.

            In dreams I'm still the boy who listens.
Others suffer sleepless nights, others find the day
too hard to climb, but climb to summits anyway.
Think of them, betrayed by their own bones or blood,
bent inside with maladies no one else can see,
for whom merely to walk a city block would be
a woozy flight.

So I've become a spinner of yarns—
hopefully not a sower of yawns—my hearing aids,
crow's feet and specs, and all my hidden pangs and pains
pleading the Fifth before I find a fifth and pour
a neat inch at cocktail time. *Look with thine ears*,
said Lear to the world prolonging. Well, I've been there,
half-hearing my way through human mazes.

When I was a boy
I listened to men weathered and withered, withstanding all
the way they'd ducked at mortar fire or kamikazes,
and women who took my arm to make it to the car.
I chauffeured the old, cajoled them to keep up the work of living,
helped them to their doors, found keys, conveyed them

to dough-smelling kitchens, pans of foiled leftovers,
letters they'd never written, love they'd never conveyed,
whatever decay of night was left to wander in.

Now I've only to hallow their too-neglected names
with yours, goddess, each time I offer a lit candle
or swallow the pills and pride or raise my ringing glass.

Notes of a Naturalist

Today I listened to one tenured professor
whining about another tenured professor,
his voice like a mosquito stabbing my ear,
and thought, *How can I get away from here?*

The cabbie who turned the dial to Radio Hate
while I said nothing—I could not be late
for the jet that would take me very far away—
had a voice I can only compare to poison spray.

And then, of course, there appeared the Head of State,
playing to perfection the rotten, rich ingrate
ejaculating orders, bloated like a toad,
which made me doubly happy to be on the road.

BC

After the silt-green rivers, cold
and roaring over their silver rocks,
we nosed the canoe ashore and stepped
up to our knees in the freezing current.

The cabin we had seen through the trees
smoked above another canoe,
keel-up in the grass, but the door
opened and the blond Norwegians

waved us out of the rain. We lugged
our gear beneath the eave and heaved
the scraping hull up next to theirs
and went inside, shaking our ponchos.

To shelter out of the rain with strangers,
sharing a loaf of bread, butter
and raspberry jam, to make coffee
on the Primus stove and share it around

until red fingers thawed, to speak
the halting phrases of welcome and thanks,
were the first pleasures, to sleep dry
for a night before our setting out—

after nearly fifty years I feel it,
the sheltered gifts, sufficient food,
the little gestures of human speech,
the kindness in their eyes at parting.

David Mason

SECURITY LIGHT

The glow outside our window is no fallen star.
It is futility itself. It is the fear of night
a neighbor burns with, nightmare of a stubborn child.

I dreamed of chasing crows in a dark of sea fog
and no wind, the chill smell of kelp and changing things,
knowing the sea's edge and the sand met where the fish lived.

I saw the waters running out to meet the water
coming in, the small crabs lifted off their claws.
I saw the trysting place of cormorants, the cliffs

of guarded nests where eagles watched like sated kings
alive, alive at the moving sand clock of the sea
where all's dissolved, where earth itself is taken down.

THE SOUL FOX
— for Chrissy, 28 October 2011

My love, the fox is in the yard.
The snow will bear his print a while,
then melt and go, but we who saw
his way of finding out, his night
of seeking, know what we have seen
and are the better for it. Write.
Let the white page bear the mark,
then melt with joy upon the dark.

AN EARLY PRIMER

At first,
I went down
and down
into the musty
dank. One stair
at a time
I went.
Not falling,

but crawling.
There I found
my mother standing
beside the light
bulb and washing
machine. She was thin
and irked. She was fat
in the middle,
and skinny.
Mostly, she
was angry.
How stupid
of me to go
where I should
not have gone.
She was burning,

and yet
she was the safe
haven in the house.
The morning's first
light. The aroma
of the coffee and
the toast. The chauffeur
of vacuum and rag.
She carried me
and the wet
laundry up
the stairs. Hung
us out to dry.
Ironed and
folded us.
Then put us
neatly away.

THE MOLE

Only the mole truly believes
he's made a mountain.
And when he struggles out from under,
he believes he sees God,
that blinding light,
that tender warmth.
He hath granted the lowly mole
the comfort of life underground,
tunneling always toward his dreams.

The mole welcomes all
with enormous hands extended wide.
Praise God who made these mighty paws
under the brightness of heaven's stars
to do their work tilling the earth. A mole
has toiled in the soil for an eternity,
each heap emerging as an early morning
surprise. Who can say for sure
if the scruffy foothills and
the high blue mountains
aren't the mounds birthed
wholly by the passionate labors
of the burrowing mole?

Teach yourself
the handshake of a mole—
an earthy, encompassing grasp,
poking pink and callused,
like a thumb from an elegant
black-velvet glove.

SEE WILLOW
— a pantoum

At last you'll know why you came.
See willow. Feel willow.
Hold to the proof of loons.
This day is like no other.

See willow. Feel willow.
Feel the slender spirit of the reeds.
This day is like no other.
Step wisely along the stones.

Feel the slender spirit of the reeds.
Crows discuss the moon.
Step wisely along the stones.
The blue jay says *believe.*

Crows discuss the moon.
Feel wind inside the cedar.
The blue jay says *believe.*
A star descends and everything rises.

Feel wind inside the cedar.
Hold to the proof of loons.
A star descends and everything rises.
At last you know why you came.

BEFORE THE FALL

Now that we're in midsummer, my love,
   all the usual flowers are in bloom.

When the foxgloves, trillium, and creeping thyme
   flaunt their blowsy bellies, who notices

the moss that cushions the loam, or the lichen
   that arms the trunks of the pine and fir?

Let's walk through the woods quietly.
   Take my hand in silence, then let me go.

ON THE OREGON COAST IN FALL

You gather a bucketful of seashells
    shaped like ears, whorled tender cochlea. Hour

by hour, the sea yields feast and famine
    simultaneously: clusters of agates

and fields of shattered crab carcasses. You
    follow a stream strewn with agates: rough, hewn

from sandstone cliffs that give them up more easily
    than basalt bluffs. Gleaming, they lure you on

and on. But plain black rocks will also shine
    when wet. And sand fleas swarm balletically over

the dead at the water's edge, licking clean
    the innards of abandoned shells. Are they

not beautiful? A shell is most valuable
    in the fast-fading time between the death

of the animal inside and the crushing
    blows of the tide rolling into itself.

HOW THE SEA

woe woven
we are rain
wet wool weight

and weft we
wait for no
one waiting

for wreck the
rocks break no
matter what

they say you
don't know what
you don't know

how do you
do this now
do you show

me myself
long past due
the distance

between us
the distance
between two

seas I see
it clearly
tonight the

mirror through
the window
the gloom of

the year its
gloaming gleams
of glitter

the stars a
streak ribbon
of silver

the river
you see how
it runs to

the sea you
see how the
sea too is

a mirror

LIVING ALONE

I quickly accustom to living alone,
small simple meals
hummus and figs
spinach and eggs
rice, a few slices of cheese.
I no longer track
the comings and goings of not-yet adults,
piles of shoes
plates on the counter
sudden changes of mood.
There is never a full load of laundry.
The well does not run dry.
Baths are long and luxurious
hot and scented
patchouli or cedar in salt.

I lock the door at night now
like a woman who lives alone in the woods
at peace with the wolves
but not so sure of the hunters.
I slip between cool sheets
and drift into twilight sleep.
My lovers are old men,
face cradled in soft chests
of gray bristling hair,
a mirror of uncluttered want
communion of pure need.

DAWN AT THE BAY OF PIGS
— *Playa Caletón, Cuba*

Dawn at *la Bahía de Cochinos*,
the silhouette of a two-man skiff
rises in a band of light,
glides beyond the horizon.
Roosters crow in every corner.
Small dogs chase *Guanabá Real*,
Yellow-Crowned Night-Heron
wading in the quiet bay.
Feet sink into coarse sand
bathed by warm salt
in a rhythm of gentle waves.

In an hour, horse-drawn carts
laden with cabbage and papaya
will clatter through the streets
toward the open-air market.
Small girls in red skirts,
eyes shining, brown faces smiling,
will chatter their way to school.

Be careful *norteamericano*.
Cotorra o Perico.
There are Cuban Parrots
in the lost and found.

POINT BARROW

I saw this woman
Walking through the ribcage
Of a dead whale
She was flensing.

The bones were bloody
With wet blubber
As she stripped away
With her ulu knife
And put the bits
In a bucket.

And later, as the Inuit
Gathered around a blanket
And tossed her in the air,
Her mukluks dancing,
Her red cheeks full,
The whole town laughing,

I thought about the long winter ahead
When we would see
Neither sun nor moon,
And the stars would become
The clean bright bones
Of the night.

A BED OF ROSES

Like flowers planted in the wrong bed,
We sometimes fail to blossom, and instead
Wait vainly for some friendly spade
To take us where a better bed is made.

It never happens, though. The earth
Is stingy with rebirth,
And like the whims that bed the plant,
We sometimes bloom, but often can't.

Pity those that nature made
For sun that ended up in shade.
Pity hope that waits in vain.
Pity a cactus in the rain.

THE FOUR SEASONS

When I was the concierge
I had no urge to ask the spring
About its length of stay.
And the spring
Spent mornings in the garden
And slept by day
Three months and left.
She did not pay.
But left a scented note that read
"Summer will pay,"
Or so the springtime wrote.

When summer came
She traveled light
And spent long days by the pool.
Summer was no fool
And after three months fled.
"Autumn will pay"
Is what the summer said.

When autumn came
He was a melancholy guest
And spent long evenings at the bar.
Autumn tipped well
And promised to make good
As spring and summer
Said he would.
He left one night
Without his bags in tow
And said from a booth
With a trace of truth,
"Winter will pay what we owe."

Then winter came
With many bags
And promised to stay and stay.
He was quite old
And drank fine wine
And added it to his bill.
"Yes, I will pay,"
He said with a sigh
And spent long nights by the fire.
He spoke of warmer seasons fled.
"Yes, I will pay," the winter said.
And he did.

EMPATHY

I know how a barn feels
When the ridge beam sags
And the paint peels.

I know how a car feels
When the seals leak
And the muffler howls.

I know how a tree feels
When autumn winds blow
And leaves lose their grip.

I know how a man feels
When his knees grow soft
From the winter in his bones.

I know the fear of the drifting canoe,
And the waterfall
That makes no sound.

UNDERTOW

I'm running down the corridors,
      Late for my watch on the bridge,
For captain's mast, for General Quarters.
      It's winter, my face frigid:

Why is my uniform tropical white?
      Down the passageways
Of shadowless fluorescent light
      I gasp, but the view stays

Unchanged—a tunnel of painted steel.
      I'm yelling: *I did my time—*
And I resigned! This can't be real!
      But all the ladders I climb

Now lead to where the lifeboat is stored.
      The PA speakers blast:
Man overboard! Man overboard!
      The boat's being lowered. I'm last

To grab a ratline and clamber in.
      My grip slips on the line—
I hit the water. And wake: my skin
      Slick with the old brine.

BRINE

To make a monkey's paw—a fist of rope
Tight as a woven rock—a bosun mate
Must learn to work a marlin spike, to make

That jab of metal behave like his sixth finger.
As though to lasso the ship beside his, he whirls
The monkey's paw over his head like a bola,

Letting it loose to haul a line across
The chewing seas between them. He cinches the ships
Together as they mirror-sail one course—

Then fuel can be taken on and cargo swapped
Like sea stories. The only sailor allowed
To carry a buck knife, he must be quick

As a rope that wraps an arm or foot to slash
This embrace. Though he whets his blade with THC
Each time he cuts a line entwined from hemp,

A bosun mate won't be disarmed by fear
Of the master-at-arms who longs to fill his brig
Like a bong. Excuse his thought that his music moves

The sun: without his pipe shrilling loud
Enough to wake all decks, the day won't start
At reveille, won't end at lights-out.

A GOOD THING

A good thing he's retired—now the hours
Can be spent checking out what's going wrong
With his feet, his eyes, his bent body. Dour
Doctors explain his pains these days belong

To him the way experience has pressed
Its fingers into his clay: the price to pay,
A salmon lunging upstream to the end it guessed
The very first time it entered the sea.

The thoughtless effort of moving everywhere,
To even run without a twinge or cramp—
The tortoise he's become has beat the hare
Across some unwanted finish line. He clamps

Tightly the book he brings to keep from feeling
Like a prisoner on death row as he takes
A dimpled seat in the waiting room. The spring
In his step has snapped. Can the doc solder the break?

The speed of life has made a blur of his past.
He sighs at the call: *The doctor will see you now.*
He sees that one of these visits will be his last.
Before he can rise to his feet, he has to bow.

THE FOURTH BOX

They say you have four kinds of box.
Standing on the first, you can talk

To passersby, condemning the monarch
Who sets his fire to bring the dark.

If no one hears, it's time to make
The ballot box a firebreak

To block the leader's blaze. When he burns
Those paper voices to whispers, you turn

To the jury box. Perhaps a verdict
Will snuff his flames before they've licked

The pages of the law to black.
If all this fails, you're left to attack

His spreading rage with the smallest one—
The ammo box. But using a gun

Might only fan the conflagration.
So you consider: didn't this nation

At its birth arise from the char
Of a far-flung empire? Are the stars

In the flag more than bullet holes?
To murder a tyrant or the soul

Of the republic—which is worse?
Who ends up in the fifth box first?

BIRCH
— for Sharon

I think I now know
　　Why the birch will split the thin
　　Layer of its skin again
And again but rarely show

The darker wood at its core.
　　Although the bark peels
　　Back, it won't reveal
Anything more

Than another papery scroll
　　Of white. Maybe the wind
　　Believes the tree has sinned
Against it by failing to hold

The song of its travels. The streaks
　　On this bar—brown and sparse—
　　Are like a sort of Morse
That can't transcribe the peaks

Of snow and races of rivers
　　The gusts have swept across.
　　But still the birch is the voice
The wind speaks in when it shivers

The flaps of bark like torn
　　Sheet music. No matter
　　How it claws at the tatters,
The wind can't change the score.

THE MIDDLE

She looked at him: *You always hog the bed.*
He glanced up from his crossword page. *You said*
To tell you what bugged me most, so I'll unload.
You're like some kind of glacial tumbleweed,
Rolling closer and closer to my side

Till I'm nearly pushed off the edge. It showed
He loved her, he said, and smiled as he always did,
Shrugging slight as a twitch. *You've tried to kid*
Your way out of any argument we've had.
You know, when you fly off on business, I'm glad:

I finally get to sleep in the middle. His head
Began to shake as if he were amazed
She'd complain about so small a thing. He promised
He'd quit—he'd stay on "his half" as best he could.
She frowned: *Your promising won't do any good.*

He'd always been a promising guy, he grinned.
You act like everything's a joke: I'm mad
Enough already. With another twitch, he raised
His hand straight as a stop sign and replied
He'd really try. One night, when he hadn't rolled

Against her, she sighed: *At last.* Near dawn, she stretched
Out her arm toward him—the skin of his felt cold.
After, she touched the depression he had made
So close to hers. Then touched the middle. She rolled
Away from it and settled on her edge.

THE BUS DRIVER'S WIFE

A water glass, his socks, the shirt he shirked—
her hands pick up the route he's slowly thrown
around. She gets he hates the weeks he worked,

the stop-to-stop people he drove to town,
their "sad sack" tales of why they can't pay fares,
the stream of copper pennies rolling down

the nowhere aisle. To fill his emptied core,
he swears: *God damn, fuck this.* But then he sees
her slump against the door, how words can pare

away her skin into such raw debris.
Not mad at you, he says. *Just mad.* So lost
in red coronas that he can't pry free.

A BARRACK'S WINDOW, INSIDE

— Minidoka

Picture two girls—
in Peter Pan collars,
bangs banging
foreheads, bouncing
on cots. Chatty,
chins cocked, they chant
jump-rope jingles,
joining their hands.
Seventy summers
swept by. Streaks
of gray grizzle
these great-aunts.
Sister, what did
we see? Sagebrush!
Barracks, blankets,
pot-belly stove.
Same, same. Even now,
you sneeze like me—
long sniff, then snort.
Bathroom's stinky.
The desert—all dust—
dammed Pa's mouth.
Thirsty. Tepid
water in tin mugs.
Nothing was nice
or clean. Nightfall—
black-haired babies
bawled all the time.
Wind wiped away.
Now who is who?

A BARRACK'S WINDOW, OUTSIDE

— Minidoka

Not meant to last,
　　　　　the mean molding
is slats of wood
　　　　　set side by side
while tar-paper
　　　　　panels have peeled.
All nailed with nine
　　　　　quick strokes. Knotty
pine boards patrol
　　　　　the porch, protect
against glary
　　　　　glass-eyed glances.
Windows widen
　　　　　at the top. The wind
blows in brown bits
　　　　　of sagebrush, night's
ill-starred islands
　　　　　of indigo.
Outside, night owls
　　　　　might dream—observe
sunset's slow
　　　　　sink into shadow.
Lanterns burn low.
　　　　　Guards call: *Lights out!*

THE OUTER LIMITS

That Monday night at eight o'clock, my brother
clicked on the black-and-white TV. Dad played
with the rabbit ears. Mom pulled out her silver
crochet hook to twist and unravel one long thread.

Nothing she made came out right. Just when the Zanti
Misfits opened the spaceship's door, Mom wanted a fitting.
I held my arms out razor-back straight, not ready
to give my life. "Don't watch," she mumbled as yarn hung

from her mouth, "if you're afraid." Eyes shut
tight, I still felt the creature's high-pitched voice
creep up my skin. As the scratchy wool met
my neck, I started to sing "Three Blind Mice"

so loudly, all I saw was Mickey, Jerry, and Mighty
Mouse scampering far ahead of me. But the alien,
a giant ant, had human eyes. "Naughty
girl," it teased: "I'll sneak under the door when

you sleep." My wavering blocked the set. Dad's hiss
of "*Get down*" drove me to the sofa. I wished
I could be a baby folded in Mom's arms. Across
the room, the screen flickered as an Army jeep crashed

through a window. Mom sniffed, "It'll be over soon."
That's when I knew I'd been betrayed. Her stitching came
more quickly. In her bumpy loops of yarn, I saw a million
insects lined up to invade our home.

THOSE LEFT TO TELL: FOR A.C.

The Igbo of Nigeria believe
you're only gone when the last relative

who remembers you has died. Dear cousin,
we're old enough to recall Grandma's kitchen—

the Nehi bottles of orange fizz lined up
for special meals on New Year's with the shrimp,

those stiff translucent shells we snapped in half.
Her sink was wide and deep—big enough

to wash my sister in. Fifty years:
the largest anniversary picture

barely held us all while our numbers
quickly spread like ripples fanning far

from shore. Only Aunty Meri
lives on; my mom, your dad—a fading story

that holds huge holes we'll never fully know.
Memory makes of us brief cameos.

GHAZAL FOR A SISTER

The house sips rain this quiet night.
No need for fame this quiet night.

Morocco's sweets; memory's mosque:
Chanting claims that quiet night.

A teapot hoards the blue of eyes.
White bones remain this quiet night.

A suicide's tomb: wet leaves and moss.
Beauty—no blame—this quiet night.

I keep your bowl, your good
book. I speak your name this quiet night.

FORGIVEN

He killed a man
and you forgave him that.
He robbed you of your father
whose only offense
was a broken brain.
Did he have the right?
Was he justified?
Did you feel guilt
for the way your father died?
He murdered the man
who loved and coddled you
all your life.
The bullet through his throat
defiled
all the cherished moments
you had shared.

Blood splattered walls,
congealed upon the floor—
a horror he left
for you to find
the day he killed

himself.

CROSSING

Far from the paddocks of restraint
where feral ponies spook and whirl
concealed in clouds of smoking dust
enthused with freedom's primal power,
the whistled throat of the iron horse
filters through the birdsong breeze.
Uncertain of its muzzled tone
eyes rein northward up the track
where shimmering ferrous stripes vibrate
with crashing of a thousand hooves.
From steaming throat the great beast cries,
bursts into our trembling space,
crushes us with heat and fear
back from the slash of spinning limbs.

The rocking wagons whinny past
dopplered down the shrinking way.
The flailing tail whips swiftly through
the closing avenue of air
as silver strings combine and fade
and silence floods the shaken grade.

LANTERN FESTIVAL

— Mojave Desert

Paper lanterns seed the sky with hope,
curtain the curve of space like fireflies
speckling the milky ways of remembering.
Ghostly glowing eyes of the departed
ascend to conflicting afterworlds
that confound our perception of peace.
Souls—snatched by swollen rivers,
charred by fierce forest fires,
shredded by salvos of hate,
of children flayed by bombs—
all float from our consciousness
into a silent sanctuary
that dampens the desolation of distress.

We come to celebrate,
we come to pray,
see spirits born by paper prisms
rise like a jeweled veil
from the embers of loss.

We come to grieve.

Jean Syed

On Children's Television

Renfrew of the Mounties, in your gray coat,
Galloping around on a fiery steed,
My first boyfriend, on you I sometimes dote.

In black-and-white, the nine-inch screen remote
Which harmed my eyes, you challenged each misdeed.
Renfrew of the Mounties, in your gray coat

On children's television, the truth I note:
Your coat was red, monochrome does mislead.
My first boyfriend, on you I sometimes dote.

You were my handsome hero, but to devote
My love when color came to supersede,
Renfrew, you were gone with your gray coat,

Square-jawed he-man. Later, did you bloat,
Did you have a paunch, were you bow-kneed?
My first boyfriend, on you I sometimes dote,

You five-o'clock starlet. Now I promote
You in this black-and-white for all to read.
Renfrew of the Mounties in your gray coat,
My first boyfriend, with puppy-love I dote.

NIGHTMARE

Quite light the chamber and in my underwear
Or maybe naked, I see a hangman's noose
Descending from a gibbet. I mount the stair
To the scaffold, protest at my ill-use,
And just then, before the long drop, I think
This is a nightmare. I'm with my mate in bed,
Comfortably. How dare my mind hoodwink
Itself. I will not die, my sleepyhead.

Although suppose what I think urges me
To capture the nightmare—for this I fear—
My husband might say I'd died from old age,
Yet I know now it would be long-lasting rage
And fright on the bed that forms my bier
And that my thought had staged the killing slowly.

Jean Syed

MY CHILDHOOD JERUSALEM

And was Jerusalem builded here,
Among these dark Satanic Mills?
— William Blake

My clattering clogs climb the bridge:
The steam-train lugs with its tonnage,
No fairer than the long chimneys
Of mills, stone row houses, foundries.
It comes, it comes, the sublime fume,
The gray-white jet of somber plume

Along the valley of my town
And which is to the English known
For cold and rain and damp and grind.
Southerners think we're unrefined,
Look down their noses as we meet,
But what comes up my nose—a treat.

The train beelines over the rails,
Its fury inhales and exhales,
Clickety-clack, in clouds of hell
Its coals fire up the acrid swell:
It grabs my breath, goes down my spine,
And dark Jerusalem's divine.

Jean Syed

HOPE BECOMES DESPAIR

I hear Handel's *Messiah* year after year
In churches, concert halls which I've forgot.
The libretto's in words I should revere
Except I have a poor view of the plot.
The rejected hero surmounts his grief,
So vile man could exile mortality.
Sure! I would like to suspend disbelief,
Go on a magic carpet fleetingly,

But it's because of the music! Were you,
Handel, living today, I'd be a fan.
Your *Messiah* should be an Emmy revue,
Or have an Oscar, or the *Palme d'Or* in Cannes.
However, outside, in the hapless air,
My mind returns, and hope becomes despair.

THE CAT AND THE LION

I have a magnificent lion—
On a Persian rug it sits,
Being stuffed and no scion
Of snarling vertebrates.

When my son paid his overdue call,
His cat visited too
But wouldn't get out from her hold-all:
A frozen, scared statue.

Yet when he stroked the lion's ear
She looked on him with awe
And emerged trustfully, no fear,
With clipped claws nudged its paw.

COMFORT CAT

Because he doesn't have a spouse,
He has me, the cat, instead.
I sit beside him in the house
And spring onto the twin-sized bed.

A loving wife would give him food,
But I am Stella, a stalking dam,
To give a sparrow that's been chewed.
This is what I do, for this I am!

I don't know why he doesn't like it,
But I'm too weak for pigs and cows,
For he could eat this like a cutlet,
This act of love with pleased meows.

For love is what he thinks about,
In sleep, at work, when he comes home,
And I comfort him without
Minding lack of shower or comb.

A VALENTINE FOR DARBY

Why do I love you, my potbellied love?
Not for your pregnant form or shiny pate.
Were those on tender those decades ago
Would I have been so indiscriminate
As to let you win my heart? No princess
From passion ever took a frog to mate.
Stout prince, could you have left the starting post
Or come within a glimpse of our first date

If you had but foreseen my sagging bust,
Those peevish lines beneath my witch's eyes?
The magic is, though coronets show rust
And threadbare rags make tatters of disguise,
Uncracked diamond, your constancy
Honors, flatters, and seduces me.

WILL WORK FOR BEER

No one knew what breed of dog it was,
a "bull" something over-engineered,
a waste of strength with too much neck and jaw,
the kind of dog they send home with a note
that reads *does not play well with other dogs,*

still undecided if it's man's best friend.
It sat beside a man who held a sign
drawn in crayon, that read "Will work for beer."
The candor, meant to be disarming, failed;
there was no work, not for beer or money,

and drivers waiting for the light to turn
felt small, but locked their car doors anyway.
The man stroked the sleek, muscled head;
his fingers, stiff and thick, seemed only fit
for grasping, making fists, and petting dogs.

With each stroke it raised its head to meet
his touch, the yellow eyes shut with pleasure.
A lap dog in an SUV yapped at them,
a furry ball with runny eyes that bounced
against the windows, brave behind the glass;

the homeless dog barely pricked its ears.
Tonight, in his dreams, he would chase the toy
and twitch and whimper in his sleep; for now
he let his stomach do the growling and sat
in bliss beneath the soiled, empty hand.

THE SCENT OF CEDAR

— Remembering John T. Williams, 1960-2010

He coaxed small totem poles
from cedar limbs he carved
with a simple folding knife.

The stacked eagles and ravens,
the beavers and wolves all in balance.
His hands were steadied

by ancestors who smoothed
his tremors long enough
to bless his work and see

him stagger on his way
and killed by four bullets
from a jumpy cop.

Most saw him a lost soul,
but he called himself *free spirit.*
We wondered—free from what?

The tyranny of socks,
the oppression of pillows,
another week in detox?

He had a family
and a song we did not know.
We cannot fully mourn him.

He was Nuu-chah-nulth.
The ancients of his tribe
were proud of him, yet wept.

He sat cross-legged and freed
the spirits trapped inside
the wood. The chips fell

around his worn Adidas
while the scent of cedar
sweetened the Seattle air.

HUMMINGBIRD

A blur shot through the open door,
through the house and slammed against
the window. As it reassumed
its mortal shape, it lay there stunned,
like a moth splayed on the sill.
I cupped it in my hands and rushed
to her room eager to play
Guess what I have?
I don't know, she said, while she brushed
her hair, *a hummingbird?*

Too bad I didn't take the time
to contemplate its weightlessness,
to look it in the eye, adore
its iridescent ruby throat.
I held an altar in my hands
but failed to worship at it,
too intent to play a child's game
and then too quickly let it go.

Donald Kentop

LUNCHING WITH LENIN

The man looks small eating lunch at Lenin's feet
as the great heroic bronze leans into the future.
The worker in his shadow reads a book and feeds
himself absentmindedly, except the street is not
Nevsky Prospekt, the lunch is not *kolbasa*, pickled
beets, and *kvass*. Instead, he munches carrots, tofu,
tacos, and green tea, both at home beneath Seattle skies.

When tourists visit, some are not amused
until their hosts explain the wryness of it all;
there is nothing to fear. Then they get it, relax,
and pose for photographs. As for nighttime partiers
between the pubs, they pay no mind. Some are fresh
from open mics, others horse around. Not born
until the Slovaks pulled him down, they laugh,
oblivious to history.

A placard tilted near the giant shoes supplies the context.
It tells you everything you need to know,
how it's worth its weight in bronze, artistic merit,
provenance, the czarist oppression, and Lenin, in fine print,
not as bad as Stalin.

What if Slovaks landed here and pulled him down again?
Would we raise him up, rededicate him,
melt him for cash, or let him lie there on his face?
It would tell us more about ourselves than him,
a test we take each time we pass him by
and flunk each time we fail to shudder.

MISS PACKHAM'S GARDEN

Watch your step going down, the stones are loose.
Edgar took a dreadful spill right here, poor man.
I mean to have them mended, but never get to it.
Had I known a garden's so demanding, I'd have
taken up watercolor instead.

Do you like it? Before you say, look again.
Notice anything unusual, not right?
O, never mind, you're too polite for candor, come
along. Since I prefer gentle introductions,
I'll introduce you to the sound of *Baby's Breath*.

Say it with me: *Baby's Breath*, the very name's
a sigh. Next is *Pussytoes, Poppy Mallow*
and *Love-in-a-puff*, of course. *Woolly Blue Curls*, you know,
there's *Gayfeather, Maiden's Hair*, and all the rest,
but names are not enough, they must be sounded, be expressed.

Of course, botanically they're quite dissimilar.
By necessity they're not arranged by size
or climate, color, scent, if they prefer to face
the north or south, but rather, how they please the ear
and how the name rolls around inside the mouth.

In contrast we have *Cat's Claw* and *Parrot's Beak*
and *Needle Grass* planted here with *Cupid's Dart*,
and juxtaposed, the sanguinates, like *Bleeding Heart*,
Bloodleaf, Blood Grass, Blood Lily, and *Silver Spear*,
my weak attempt at irony . . . you have the idea.

This bed's my favorite, planted just so I could say
Plumbago, Sassafras, Squill, and *Cushion Bush,*
Kumquat, and *Chickabiddy.* There's St. Francis watching
over *Elephant* and *Lamb's Ears, Lion's Tail,*
Wolf's and *Leopard's Bane,* and *Birds of Paradise.*

A *Rosary Vine* grows at his feet with Jerusalem Sage
and *Mary's Tears,* and *Voodoo Lilies,* just in case.
There's much to do, but first, let's rest here on the bench.
Edgar's bringing tea, but did you know, I plan to dig
the garden up and replant everything in French?

'Quietly, without excuse, . . .'

Quietly, without excuse, my heart
decides to improvise and runs a riff
of double rolls and ruffles. The solo puts

me on my back, and once again I glide
beneath the alternating ceiling tiles
and fluorescent lights. Here, routines rule.

I am swaddled in protocol
and comforted to know my crisis
is someone else's day at work.

YOUR TEA KETTLE'S PANTOUM

The house holds me, rising early
as you sleep; I follow my feet
into the kitchen, turn on the light
over the stove and the coffee maker

as you sleep; I follow my feet
out, back, see by the light
over the stove and the coffee maker
a shadow on the floor;

out, back: see by the light
the hieroglyph
a shadow on the floor,
a handle in a circle

the hieroglyph,
a constellation of yours—a stepping stone,
a handle in a circle
to you: your tea, your stove

a constellation of yours—a stepping stone
and kettle—keeps me as I cross
to you; your tea, your stove
steeping me in our days where

the kettle keeps me as I cross
into the kitchen, turn on the light
steeping me in our days where
the house holds me, rising early.

Victoria Ford

A STAND OF COLLECTIVES
— November 2016

a cumulonimbus of facts
a gasp of votes
a wobble of certainties
a dustpan of regrets

a link of complacencies
a hacking of trusts
a hard drive of entitlements
a spreadsheet of thieves

a remembrance of doors
a sidewalk of options
an aspiration of stepladders
an endurance of cobblestones

a breath of senses
a room of bridges
a morning of hands
a street of freedoms

AN ARC OF COLLECTIVES
— November 2017

"I do not pretend to understand the moral universe; the arc is a long one, my eye reaches but little ways; I cannot calculate the curve and complete the figure by the experience of sight; I can divine it by conscience. And from what I see I am sure it bends towards justice."
Theodore Parker (1810-1860)

a career of inches
a stance of miles
a hush of maps
a library of flashlights

a gloom of windows
a practice of mornings
an unbending of mirrors
an elevation of planets

a breath of mothers
a marathon of men
a palm of birdseed
a plan of stars

SLOW BLUE

As time's canopy
where the cut tree shivering
slightly can appear

stopped: that blink eon
before stupendous motion,
so this saurian

slow blue, the heron,
when the breast muscle ignites
its deep furnace here,

and the tidepool soughs
and stirs, and the long eyelid
of the wing lifting.

DAY MOON

Only look askance. Can't
see it otherwise. Crescent
on the wrought sky-sconce—

flakelike paring—moth-
wing—windscreen with wet petal—
glacial tablecloth's

crisp fabric cobwebbed
in what icewater-pitchers
aclink with icecubes

do: *that* hyaline,
membranous skirting, unsquare
whirl, linen alive

with it, the flicker-
of likening, the not-there
of it, the for-lack-

of-words delighting,
blue future's egg-tooth, truth, the
candle in daylight.

EASTER WINGS

Where else but Airport
Security, coffee-deprived, bored?

Under Hermes,
my graduate students assure me

poetry is characterized—
terrorized,

one might say—by what they menacingly
call semantic indeterminacy,

or instability, or contingency,
or chance.

Usually they call it *disjuncture.*
Unsure

of what they mean exactly, I prove it,
removing

my shoes.
What shows

on the full-body scan—
no wish to imagine.

The whole security line's a campus
akimbo

with collegiality. It's mid-semester;
most are

flying off to copulate
in Mexico. Good plan! Our pilots

arrive carrying briefcases. They skirt
Security,

flashing badges,
unsuspicious.

I am deemed no Saracen.
On a blaring TV, Risen

Christ is advertised:
I infer

Easter. Agnostic,
I believe in no hand on the joystick.

Instability characterizes the situation.
Wishing

it away, I infer
fear

and wonder about its half-life.
Lufthansa lifts off

under me. The set sun disinters,
a fanned cinder.

The Pacific Plate aches north another inch.
Ancient Japan leaks cesium into her grandchildren.

The saltwater
is contaminated with tears.

NECESSITY

Re: *rain*, and the long theological stalemate
concerning its origins, a tale Talmudic

in nuance, Homeric in scope: this was classic Lachrymism
vs. vulgar Micturism, paired like the chromosomes

of our tradition. At stake: the nature of Heaven.
At issue: the source of life, in rain. In the event,

the conclusive stroke was dealt by the geochemists,
who by the closing years of the last century had amassed

data demonstrating the identity of rain and tears
to the 97th part, in a theorem which survived rigorous peer

review. By contrast, undistilled urine assayed
as correlative only to the 60th part, notwithstanding acid

precipitates, adjusted mathematically, allowing for a salt-
correction constant. The question was settled.

Of course, rear-guard Micturian die-hards and tenured
professors with careers at stake and minds too inured

to the old way of thinking continued to cavil. Attempts
to impeach experimental procedure failed. Die or adapt:

the science proved solid. And we were happy, were we not?
Sure, though Heaven knows one cannot count on Nature

to conform to human preference, none could deny
a private relief at the proof: the tragic mind of Adonai

might henceforth be petitioned. The vulgar Eiron
was cast down. Earth bloomed. Heaven wept pure thereon.

≋

The droughts began in the second decade following.
Crops failed in successive seasons. Fields lay fallow.

We attempted public supplications, under open skies,
the sadness of our plight sharpened by rhetors, our cries

drawn taut by singing masters, our kennings
pitched by poets to the asymptote of pity, razor-keen.

Still God withheld His tears. We sacrificed.
We burned barns, livestock, houses, towns. We revisited

more ancient screeds. With stricken reluctance
unimaginable to any human not so fated, we looked

into the red eye of necessity and agreed to begin
sacrificing the children again.

≋

We will not be judged. Our lamentations exonerate us. Arraign
ineluctable fact in the court of the real. Physics

was never of our choosing. We must have rain
or die. One must live in the world as it is.

EKPHRASIS

A traveler to an island city-state
(grant faith to this utopian travelogue)
tells of a wondrous statue in a bay
wiped innocent each morning by the fog.
Nearby, seeking refuge from the waves,
apartment towers perch on staggered stilts
and two grinning figures cast in bronze
surmount a base sunk deep into the silt—
the linked arms of industrialist brothers
whose carbon fortunes fueled a dual aplomb.
Their specs glimmering like Morgan dollars,
their plinth's inscription too would glean claptrap
were it not for the waves lapping their collars:
"Pulled up by our very own bootstraps."

VILLANELLE FOR VILLAINS

The earth beneath our feet keeps changing tactics,
shifting as the sea recalls the sand.
You want to live, they call you a fanatic.

PSE sees green in hawking fracked gas
pumped from poisoned wells on stolen land.
The earth beneath our feet keeps changing tactics.

Tacoma City Council Members back this
backyard bomb, constituents be damned.
We want to live, they call us all fanatics.

Water Warriors rise, activists get active;
in solidarity we make our stand.
Steadfast protectors, ever-changing tactics.

Puyallup salmon breach endangered status
as keystone spirits battle corporate scam.
You want to live, they call you a fanatic.

Macquarie Group's Nick Moore rings Kimberly Harris:
Why's LNG not moving as we planned?
The earth beneath their feet has changed its tactics
where living waters gather, furious and fanatic.

PUYALLUP ESTUARY

In the bay, everything returns.
Kelp bends to waves' fleeting words,
then turns its yearning southward soon as water
brims the shore. So too unmoored life:
Salmon track the scent of ancestors;
Heron chart stars; Orcas circle

the Salish Sea as legends circulate,
evolving so when tale at last returns
to teller's ear, it is the ancestors
who through a stranger's rough-hewn words
reveal their familiar selves. If life
leapt from the sea, it's fitting that to water

we should in fits return. And so the water-
front revs and throbs, the traffic circle
clogged with preening cars, bay choked with boats: young life.
When reincarnation's served, I'll take my turn
in any castoff shell that can skip leeward
over youth's brash certainty its ancestors

have nothing new to say. What would those ancestors
think of this scene upon the water?
I can't say. Nor have I yet found words
equal to the threat of the concentric circles
the Port Commission's painted on our back. I turn
toward the LNG refinery, a shrine to life

rendered into fumes of profit: life
drained, filled, and flensed; ancestors
denied the just and natural return
of fins and fronds and bones to living water,
living air, and living soil; a circle
broken sure as greed sheers sense from words.

I walk on ground that colonizers' words
have poisoned. Yet injured land still harbors life,
dead language bears truth's embers. Encircled
by cupped hands and breathed to light, ancestral
spirit liberates the slag heaps. Water
protectors greet us prodigal kin returning

to hold the circle by these sacred waters
where we keep to living beings our human word
until we join earth's ancestors in our turn.

MARCO POLO RETURNS

When Marco returned
the city was larger.
People noticed his spices
that improved their meals.

Soon tired of stories
on alien culture,
they queried instead
on weapons and trade.

As soon as he could
Marco wrote it all down,
got dressed before dawn
and slipped out of town.

Derek Sheffield

THE SKOOKUM INDIAN

— since 1921, Wenatchee, Washington

Above the Dollar Tree those dark eyes
shift side to side all day and all night.
Now and then one of them winks.

He's a giant motorized head, this Indian of ours,
with a cartoon nose and long black braids.
Above the Dollar Tree those dark eyes

shadow the changing lights wherever we drive,
googly holes pinned to a wobbly sky
where now and then one of them winks.

A grin big as a sunset that won't die
promises a brand of apples long dead
beside the Dollar Tree. (Those dark eyes.)

We mostly forget, but those red cheeks
plump the photos of posing out-of-towners.
Now and then one of them winks

back. His name means *strong* or *monstrous*.
The tilt of his single feather never alters.
Above the Dollar Tree those dark eyes:
now and then one of them winks.

EMERGENCY

A doe sets her left
front hoof onto
the road as I roll
to a stop—and
watch her through
the windshield take
a second sleek
step as another
doe appears. More
slow steps, and
pause as they turn
dark, unblinking
eyes toward two
cars pulling up
behind me.
A few seconds
is all it takes—
the deer going on,
nearly there,
my foot lifting
from the brake—when
two others appear
and the glint
of another car.
And I press
my foot more
firmly to the brake—let

them be one
thing ahead of
ours—and let us
get where we need to
watching the silky
pistons of their steps,
my hazard lights
pulsing like a
cornered heart.

TRAVELING AGAIN THROUGH THE DARK

— for Bill and all

Having flown from their far cities
and checked in downtown, the ecopoets
gather at the university to elucidate
the nature of this new nature poetry.

One taps her mic, "Can you hear me?"
and they are off with a talk that leads them
from the faces of Personification Peak,
down a road that curls along the curves

of Mimesis Creek and corkscrews them
ever deeper: "I really hate that poem
where the speaker runs over a deer
and gets out to find she's pregnant—

you know that one?" Many heads nodding.
"It's when he says, 'I thought for everybody.'"
"What hubris!" says another. "Why's he thinking
for *me*?" And after a third agrees—frowning

through his goatee—they work as one
to shove the poem out of their consideration.

Derek Sheffield

APRIL

Now he closes his book.
Slanting light warms
a blue bowl of napkins,
a table specked with crumbs.
He closes his eyes.

Birds. Passing car.
All the leaves lengthening
in their own good time.
Somewhere a bear
opening her eyes.

It is enough today
to walk upstairs
where his daughter curls
in her pink blanket.
It is just right

to bend close and sniff
the lotion of her sleep
and read in the lines
creasing her neck
their once upon a time.

AUBADE

He woke and slipped into sleeves in the dark. A few steps
creaked. Clink of spoon as he stirred cream. Made sure
not to trip, the toy prince sprawled by the door.
Left that sleeping house like a thief. Still
our girl woke, she says, hours later

while they talk on the phone,
the sun outside beating its gong.
He can hear how it must have
gone, that little voice rising
through the dark room,

"Is it morning time?"
as the window held
the lights of his car

sweeping away
under star scatter.

FIRST HALLOWEEN

In the parking lot of a church,
cars and trucks raggedly circle
a great bonfire. *Good fun,*
said the family who invited us

to these vampires and zombies
and their parents making their way
through the flickering orange light.
A chubby black cat walks up

to one of the tables and says to a clown
what we have just taught her to say,
what all the witches and monsters
around her are saying,

and in return he gives her a question
she does not know how to answer.
He holds a piece of hard candy
wrapped in cellophane

next to his red grin, his red ball
of nose, and chants again: *If you really
want a treat, answer my question, oh so sweet,
why oh why did Jesus have to die?*

She looks up to us where we stand,
as wordless as she is.
She has been trying on this night
for weeks, going from princess

to fairy to an hour ago when we drew
whiskers across her cheeks
and pinned a tail to her diaper.
She does the only thing she knows to do—

she holds out her pumpkin bucket.

SECRET OF THE BONFIRE

We went walking on the beach,
Dad of fifty, daughter twelve.
A millennium of wind-blown waves
Washed the selfies from ourselves.

A seal nosed up a shiny ball,
The mallards turned their heads to sleep.
Kite surfers cut out zip line wakes
Across the surface of the deep.

O Jack o' lantern of the sun,
O candelabra of the moon—
No sooner said than (smile) undone—
The cart before the hearse cartoon.

How many skeletons in the closet?
How many Presidents in the lie?
How many special prosecutors
To stoke the first indictment's *fie*?

What's a boondoggle? asks the girl
Whose earbuds thump with saving face.
Is doggerel a greenhouse gas?
The wilting world spins on apace.

A bonfire is a sordid boon
Said the patient to the evening sky.
And a daughter grows up way too fast—
No bones about it, standing by.

ATMOSPHERIC RIVER

Happy hour passes
Without distinction. Wind, rain—
Wet leaves clogging drains

In every street.
Oh, the faces that you meet
Between Sturm und Drang.

The argument went
Nowhere. Nor could we recall
Who said what to whom.

One minute there was
Teething, the next an albatross
Hanging in the room.

REFLECTION

What is the self?
The dinner I just ate?
The four-part novel on the shelf?

Evidently, it's late—
the self looms large
beside the empty plate.

There are batteries to recharge
and lessons to prepare.
I scribble midnight marginalia

in volumes two and three. The air
is full of cell-
phone grievance everywhere
self is, if not self-aware.

LULLABY FOR MIDDLE AGE

Fog becomes a frost
Bog turns into bile
Fasting grows fastidious
Walking off the miles.

Friends all end up frowning
Clowns make awful clones
Clams raise quite a clamor
Hawking megaphones.

I becomes an other
Child grows up to be
A version of her parents
Voting absentee.

Travel sprouts an armchair
Mortgage springs a leak
Tongue ties itself in slip knots
Parsing doublespeak.

Trade winds change direction
Money changes hands
Sunlight changes everything
An earthworm understands.

Gun shows open loopholes
Legislators stall
Bedtime comes too quickly
Or doesn't come at all.

Frost outlines a feeling
Chalk outlines a man
Deluge washes handshakes
Making planetary plans.

BIRD NOTE

Pacific wren,
You stack up well
(Counting swell by swell)
Against an agitated ocean.

So small, so flush
With pique,
Well-versed in summary-critique:
A squall, no less, crashing through the underbrush.

Rick Clark

LOVE & NATURE: SENRYU

beach walk—
the whole family leans together
into the wind

≋

so much talk of guns—
I find all his doors unlocked
in the dead of night

≋

the cabin's deck chairs
unmoved after last weekend's
argument

≋

wilderness lake jag—
turning into a financial
consultation

≋

father and son
carving first hiking sticks—
troubled by knots

≋

camped up river
all summer—the survivalist
never stops talking

≋

dizzying footbridge—
a shoe tossed for a joke
on a mossy cliff

≋

the new young lovers—
wrestling a used mattress
up the bottom steps

≋

rearview mirror—
the lovers catch each other
chewing their nails

≋

plate tectonics—
Sam and Cate are breaking up
in the sidewalk

Author's Note: The senryu is close cousin to the haiku
(both are Japanese verse forms), with the same syllable
and line concerns but focused on human folly rather
than on nature. Traditionally speaking, senryu do not
need to make a reference to the seasons. Typically,
English language haiku (ELH) poets (strive to) write
haiku and senryu in fewer than seventeen syllables,
since Japanese, which is a syllabic language, requires
more syllables to say what we might say in English,
which is a phonetic language.

BIRD HAIKU, IN SEASON

Spring

the song sparrow—
not exactly groomed
for the big aria

≋

a barred owl
casing a robin's nest—
so hum

> Author's Note: "*So hum*" is a breathing mantra that, in Sanskrit, means "That I am." Intone "*So*" ("That") inwardly on inhaling and "*hum*" ("I am") on exhaling, attuning to the sounds, words, and meaning—finding a rhythm. I would call this the breath of acceptance.

Summer

loses a few feet
shaking the lake from her wings—
an osprey

≋

in the mallard world too—
the drakes guffawing
in tight circles

Fall

a small bird chirps
out in the autumn rain—
what I meant to say

the one-legged sparrow—
still embraced by the clan
on the power line

Winter

traffic rolling by below
a hawk slowly plucks
a woodpecker

wingtips stitching
the glassy cove a scoter
whistles away

"wingtips" composed with Geoff Clark, brother

COME AGAIN?

No matter where I go I think of somewhere
else, some place I've traveled in the past.
In Morocco, breathing dry Saharan air,
I saw Sonora with its cactus and its dust.

If every single place must have its double
and every double doubles-up the same,
then here, with my elbows on this table,
I could still be anywhere but where I am.

THE PHILOSOPHY OF THE MOTEL POOL

After the travelers have all gone to bed,
the motel pool settles into its blues.
The filter motor goes quiet, and the water
stops moving. Everyone who has been there
was just passing through. Empties and ashtrays,
candy wrappers, someone's lost flip-flops
or tank top or towel or fashion magazine—

in the soft glow from the underwater lights these
things lie around the deck like fragments of dreams,
bits of evidence at a crime scene,
but the pool itself is unperturbed.
The woman who swam laps early
and the man who stopped to watch her
are both gone. The family of four from Omaha,

the honeymoon couple, silly with champagne,
and the boy who played frogman all afternoon
will not be back again. No matter who dives in,
no matter how they splash or agitate,
every night the pool resolves
to be flat, placid. It is not depressed.
It's only doing what water does at a time like this.

MORGAN STREET JUNCTION CAFÉ, 4 PM ON MONDAY

Wild five-year-old kids tumble in the chairs.
The adolescent girl reads away the afternoon,
avoids her home and everything that's there.
Each of us has a debt to pay the weather.
Today is gray as a movie of London,
greasy-haired people in buildings of old
black brick and sooty windows Dickens spoke
to the world. And who spoke you, old woman,
newspaper trembling in your hands? Or you,
trying to overhear a conversation so quiet
you think you tumbled into a forest of vespers?
Bars exhale their patrons, the street
trebles like a song, and inside every house
when one light switches off, another comes on.

VENETIAN VILLANELLE

She is a mother first, in every church
she lights a candle for her harrowed son.
One already lit supplies the match.

Today *San Stefano*, above her arched
a heaven of dark keel vaulting. Here, an icon,
Byzantine, true presence in the church

of the second Eve, the mother she beseeches.
She drops a euro in the box. It rings
numbly. Someone's loss will be her match.

Who sees one candle add to a brightened niche,
calling out to Mother, Father, Son?
We're none of us at home. In every church

bright fields of candles. We are Croesus rich
in grief, God knows—Romans killed his son.
Whose candle is she using for a match?

Who would love a god who isn't wretched,
knowing what it means to lose a son?
His son returned, we learn in every church.
She asks her son to be a perfect match.

ANOTHER NEIGHBOR

*— for Will Stacey, killed in Afghanistan
by an Improvised Explosive Device ("IED")*

Flags scramble up the wall
past flowers neighbors leave, and cards.
Will in a ballcap. *Remember the Fallen.*
The bittersweet in his parents' yard.

Spring can rustle Latin in the leaves,
a *dulce et decorum est,*
susurrus of his neighbors' love.
Then days of blow-back, stupidity, and waste,

not him, but the war he fought.
His motives multiplied on site,
reopening the schools grim beards had shut,
for the kids, *against* the benighted.

The son of teachers, he'd resisted school.
Might he teach? A marine, he'd learned to lead—
even as his squad moved single-file,
lest someone trip an IED.

A FRIEND

His half-pulled punch said he didn't buy
the memory I'd recovered to explain
myself. *You know that memory lies*
so seamlessly. Better to trust the pain.

He was alone in this, as most had said
how cruel, be strong, betrayal's such a blow.
Allied with the story I had made,
they comforted me, affirmed my angry woe.

My friend's words hurt, although I didn't doubt
that he'd been wrong and speaking out of love.
But from then on, when memory spoke out,
from the back of the room a hand would briskly wave.

The more that hand rose up, the more my tale
seemed off the rack, off-track, a fantasy.
Shamed into long silence when it failed,
I say this now for the friend who stood by me.

A BACKWARD GLANCE

Low tide. A muddy island packed with gulls.
In the crypt of *San Zaccaria* Mary stands

on an altar that the tides are eating. Eight doges
rest humidly in walls of unmarked stone.

Always the same and not the same, the sea
rising, the sea descending, we never see it move.

The walls are stained and mildewed a meter up.
We've entered history to watch paint dry.
We haven't done a thing and then we're gone.

AT RYOAN-JI TEMPLE

A gravel garden
raked in small waves around stones.
Islands, continents.
Old master, I see your work.
You don't even need to look.

CAPITAL

— for Salem, Oregon

River-carved city, green with leaf-light,
in you our civil law is born.
Beneath your rotunda that shoulders the sky, *accord*
calls us to set conflict aside.

Salem, we're speaking *Peace* each time
we say your name.
Salaam, shalom. At your site, our mapmakers place
a star's steady shine.

ON THE AEGEAN

When every ship had sails, the sea
was a copse of pale trees
glinting sun from their leaves.
When all ships had sails, a harbor
was the wintery arbor—
thin trunks taking a leafless ease.

EVANGELIA SINGS

— a municipal servant serenades at the pier

Those who sing by the sea
draw a breeze
that lifts white wings
of foam from the deep.

When Evangelia sings—
sitting at the pier, her office hairdo
smoothed just so, breasts and belly
in a swimsuit's silky sling—

her voice is a riffle of doves
flown down from chalky cliffs,
it's the white and white
of wings above

saltwater's wimpled hue,
it's the poet's covey of words
streaming along
this blue, green, blue.

THE GHEE-EATER

— as for the appeal of a certain avatar's
sweet, androgynous looks

He grew up on a butter so white and frothy
it fills the bowl with its cloud.
Such mounds of confection arise
from celestial cows as slender-faced and flanked
as deer with their sloe-cast eyes.

Milk can be so sweet its globules of fat
are white, not yellow, their traces on his fingertips
a mere sheen. His own milkless breasts preside
above a nipped waist. Inside his mouth rimmed with butter,
the whole universe resides.

Krishna's skin is enough blue to call him
Obscure One. That blue can grow deep enough
to divide him into as many sleepless nights
as the number of women who long to suckle him, bed him,
O Black One, Dark One, divine.

Paulann Petersen

MIDNIGHT'S FRUIT

Small sweet drupe of darkness.
Indigo's honeyed egg
laid in a nest's bramble-fray.

A blackberry erupts from a bloom
white as unexpected light, pale
as a moon's nightly sashay.

The nether hours boil down
to an inky syrup that makes
this tongue-taste of sugared shade.

THE CRUSH

You stand in a dark room and grow a tree in your chest.
The color pink is your national anthem.
You have fled the burning city, but your pocket smolders.
He bats his eyelids and dust flies.
You are a well trying to quench its thirst,
a tiger licking its bloody paw.

No eyes are on you, you are all eyes.
He is space age technology.
You are a fist filled with fingers. He is a ghost without a sheet.
You are a buzzing saw in the forest.
The only thing you have ever wanted is more.

AUBADE

She remembers how
his crotch smelled
of leather and sea salt.
For weeks she turned
down helpings
of filet mignon
or any bittersweet
concoction set to fool
her palate into thinking
the table was set
especially for her.
This was love, this
willow spring smell
of sweet grass and earth
this bouquet of exotic
flowers that lingered
long after dawn broke
the flat plate of sky.

WEBS AND WEEDS

Sidewalks of webs and weeds
Run parallel to empty lots where foul deeds
By handkerchief heads and winos were played,
To that old house where we stayed.
Irma Jean, Cora Jean and I, three debs,
Against the cracks of weeds and webs.

Sitting through matinees, dodging chores,
Chewing gum; claiming boys were bores.
But secretly grooming hair and breasts;

Jennie's brood, a female nest.
Irma, long-legged, delicious full lips,
Taught Cora and me to wiggle our hips.
George Darlington Love, a beau, my first;
They yelled his name like a tribal curse

As his virginal fingers pressed our bell.
Against that background of sights and smells,
We ignored switchblades, zip guns, and knees
Shattered by cops in that place without trees.
Now memories of dances are sprinkled like seeds
Among cousins and sidewalks of webs and weeds.

Colleen J. McElroy

IN PRAISE OF OLDER WOMEN

once when a blue finger of moonlight fell
through the window she happened upon
a neighbor asleep in the space of slats
the blinds all but obscuring the sight of him
slumbering under the moon—cock and balls
languishing ripe as fruit against his thigh
hanging in such innocence unsheathed she almost
called out fool that she was: Beware: such delicate
sights have driven more than one woman to despair
instead she watched him breathe—relishing
for a moment that secret space where night
grows soft and the moon's detumescence forgives—
and where if this jeweled light holds they might
strip themselves of years if only for one night

HAIKU & SENRYU

a curtain of spider silk lifts
in the noon breeze—
all four cats snoozing

late afternoon on the bluff
my shadow
drags me along

the autumn-red maple leaf
a potential mate
for your lost mitten

water rushes over white stones—
you laugh at nothing
I've said

sunlight wakens sheets—
I say your name to
the vacant pillow

≋

soaring to the stars—
my paper airplane
and me

≋

when we were in love,
up in the sky, a parade
of elephants

UNZIPPED VILLANELLE

I have no shame though others call it sin,
born with a hunger hushed on my lips,
I learn what I need to know through skin.

I offer sunwarm lessons of morning in
sweet shushes over bare shoulders, bare hips.
I have no shame though others think it sin.

Heavy-handed, pious women are chagrined,
withholding lush of breasts, tongue, fingertips.
I learn all I need to know through skin.

What is better than the feather-brush of mouth akin
to angel's wings smoothing your downy wisps?
I have no shame though others brand it sin.

I crave the heaving of a body readying its sloe-gin
sweetness to release in flighty, gushing sips.
I learn what I want to know through skin.

I rub and suck, tickle and lick. I raise a din,
ecstatic rushes praising my soul's lusty eclipse.
I have no shame for this favorite sin.
I love what I learn through skin.

GET UP & READ IT, REGARDLESS
— for sparsely attended events

Read a poem—to the air.
    Spare not a written (or typewritten) word

From fear
    That it go unheard.

Read a poem—to the abyss,
    As intently as (yes) I *am* reading this.

Read one to the un-listening ear,
    One that *you'd* like to hear.

Those who are gathered be few
    Or none; you need not read for *any*one.

Just *read* out-loud; enunciate well.
    Even these (grieving) the denizens of hell

Shall halt—their own lamentation,
    Turning & yearning up toward this

Oration sublime,
    Timelessly told & intoned.

The incarcerated, interred, enthroned—will
    In the Soul of their souls

Take heed of this,
    Which you needlessly read.

Present your poem to the living ground, stillness
    Enshrouded in sound.

Address the star's unblinking vault.
　　Those who ignore—do not fault.

Leave them to graze the sward.
　　(Ignorance is its own reward.)

Read a poem to unoccupied space,
　　An' trace the approval on faceless face.

Read a poem to the chair, the table, the wall,
　　With precise animation.
　　　　Read it all.

Filling this room to capacity
　　Augurs naught for your own veracity.

Nor would momentous applause
　　Likely incite more inventive a clause.

Un-parsimonious approbation,
　　Plaudits of critics in aerial station—these
　　　　Are a part of the show.

In essence, though, a show it is *not*, no—
　　Such superfluous rot.

Poesy, this primeval rite of
　　Sage's golden age twilight,

Borne to this very day, this *room*, calls forth
　　Lazarus from the dark tomb, calls us to *read*,

Not for me, nor for you—to *do*,
　　As it *is* to do. (Allow at least one poem through.)

It's your turn to pick one (blessing or curse) an' turn
      Picayune into—uni-verse.

Embody some poem, perhaps *more* than one,
      & When your poetry's done,

Content in what you have heard & have said,
      Go back home; go to bed.

CHANGE OF WORLDS
— in honor of a friend's beloved son

A loved one dies & is gone.
  The body we knew is no longer a whom

& We face that one face we've addressed—
  Is not of *this* place

But was only a guest
  Who has left an old world for a new.

Surprising to us is that *we've* done so, too.
  This is not the world it was,

When life which-is-done-here was clearly a does.
  We were fond of our world intact,

& Then hurled from that which we had by something
  Beyond us (which add or subtract).

We grieve. It is time that we grieve.
  It is human to do so, & human we are,

As we come here & (yes)
  As we leave. We grieve until grief itself die.

It rains until all of the rain
  That remains up above us give way to the sky.

& Then, at *our* end of the end,
  We simply let go of one visible friend,

Leaving room for a friendship unseen
  In the marvelous worlds

Where we've never been.

PASSION

In younger years, I read at seventy
I would be deaf to passion's siren song,
And I'd admit the possibility
If only you had never come along.

I'll let the others find serenity
In cards or golf or whiskey, neat and strong.
I much prefer excitability
Each time I see that you have come along.

All things, of course, have obsolescency
And we cannot evade that grievous wrong
So when I reach a hundred seventy
I'll turn away from passion's siren song.

IF ONLY

If only I had understood
How great the final act would be,
I'd stage it backwards if I could
If only I had understood.
I'd even claim the first scenes should
Be cut in their entirety
If only I had understood
How great the final act would be.

John Byrne

SO WHAT IF I HAVE WRIT BEFORE

So what if I have writ before
That age intensifies delight,
Which prompts the constant yearning for
Return into the promised night.

Such words are true and truth can't be
Unwelcome to an honest ear,
When much that's prattled endlessly
Maligns accumulating years.

And yet an error might exist
In early versions of this praise,
For talking but of nights will miss
The possibilities of days.

So let my message be refined:
Aged love is better all the time.

GRACE NOTE

She was a lovely sonnet
Poor i, a humble rhyme
Thistle to her violet
Shade beneath her shine.

Yet there was that between us
No genre might contain
A thing *sui generis*:
A passing, sweet refrain.

Her iambs and my dactyls
(The graceful and the crude)
Made music contrapuntal
And each the other wooed.

Within her generous pentameter
My less became her more
She welcomed my tetrameter
And whispered, *mon amour*

That beings so diverse
Could make that pairing rhyme!
My consonance was terse
Her assonance sublime.

THE MATADOR

There are talons that rend the air,
Wings whose daring brings
Measure to the open sky.

There, to the west, a thing swift as the wind
Just pierced the void between bridge struts
As pigeons burst out in a white
Chrysanthemum of clattering wings.

Mark it again, where it loops
Back through that narrow airway,
A plumed boomerang. Then,
To soar over iron bow in an ascending
Spiral path of light. Next, on kiting wings,
To trim, bend, accelerate
Like a flung stone
Toward compelling earth.

Dangerously late, wings flare like a cape,
Catching cushion of air to arrest, dodging
Flinty hooves and hooking horns of earth *Olé!*

Leveling low, wingtip to wave top,
It darts away, whose name, *peregrine,*
And eager wings, say
No lingering, till it is one
With the dark of distant water.

GREENLAKE SUNSET

Feather wafted from a height
Marks a fishing osprey's pass
Frisbee from unseen hand
Flutters down to meadow grass

Scanty-clad skaters dashing by
On speedy rollerblades
Couple strolling arm-in-arm
Join a throng in promenade

Dragonfly among the reeds
Darting in and out of view
Its fourfold wings, fine-veined and sheer
Glow with iridescent hues

Offshore, a swimmer, only seen
In arm-stroke's light-reflecting arc
Oblivious of traffic drone
A redwinged's song, tendrils of dark

Crows strung loose in evening sky
Like beads in a rosary
Set off by setting sun to roost
In distant leafy tree

Solitary figure standing
Silhouetted by the bay
Mute, reverent witness
To last light epiphany

A rose patina binds them all
The day grown grandly dim
Sun's effulgent final fugue
Flares from the western rim.

like us they are lonely

— from various articles discussing pollen discovered in the graves of Neanderthals

their stories we paint
on rock walls give breath
to hands hearts and time

the daisies we place
in place of their eyes
will brighten their way

the eyes of flowers
are always open
looking to the light

three minutes till midnight

there is a calm
before
the
boom

instigators

blame victims

boom

the world

whimpers

boom

another tomorrow
lost

boom

another bloom
burned

there are mushrooms

in the sky

beneath rolling overcast

we stand

they stand

motionless

motionless

mist
not trying
to be rain

lingers

a shiver
comes
from the sea

we watch them
watching us
watch them

some
hidden
grace

swells
inside us

watching
elk
watch us

the sea is silver
the crash and clatter
of waves
deliberate

and we walk away
not wanting

to lose

this awkward grace

SLIPPING

I squeeze myself into the tiniest opinions, like those
octopi who slip their tanks by
narrowing their bodies, wringing
their slick skin like a washcloth, then coasting down drainpipes:
Sayonara, suckers! Fair and square, they're gone.
I'm not out for a soft landing, just one
that will whisk me down-current
with mute, ruthless efficiency.
It's what I'm good at, being small.
A *slip of a thing*, they used to say and now
I really am. Catch me if you can. I'll slither
through any crevice lickety-split. It's my superpower,
to go at any time. The contortions
don't even hurt anymore. I'm a human
oil slick, lubricious and covert. Ask me anything.

WHY I DIDN'T WRITE A POEM TODAY

Because the cat caught sudden
sight of a fly, and I couldn't keep
my eyes on the screen for watching
his obstinate pursuit of this elusive,
graceful speck, straight up the screen door,
over the kitchen table, onto the windowsill and sink,
then back again for damn near forty minutes.
He didn't stop
to doubt his methods or
the worth of his pursuit. He did not lose focus
or surrender to fatigue.
Each new sighting
ignited fresh exuberance, and I thought,
lightning, and,
I've been dead a long time now.
Myself, I've been careful
for years to bury
my fires in sand each morning
before entering the glum
din of this world, and I think
of chasing ink across pages
in my own pursuit
of some agile, juicy speck,
grown rich and fat
on equal parts despair and fervor.

PERSIAN FLAW

— "Persian flaw": a minor flawed stitch sewn into a Persian rug to reflect human imperfection and devotion to God

So we will crave
the circumstance of our shame.
So we will allow
only the treacherous in. So we will do
to ourselves what was done
to us. So we will gain mastery.
So we can believe
that it was love.
So we will learn
that love is empty.
So we can become
exhausted.
So we will meet
despair.
So we will be granted
no more choices.
So there can be only
our long fall in offering.

So in the falling
we will thrash our limbs
and plead for rescue.
And in the silence that's returned,
we'll find our wholeness.
And in our wholeness, we will clasp
the broken stitch,

and in that embrace
there will be born
devotion, and in devotion
we will know our worth,
and in our worthiness
we will offer up compassion.
And in our compassion, we will find
a god in every failing.

ON FAILING TO CONTRIBUTE
TO A *FESTSCHRIFT*

"I missed my chance with one of the lords of life . . ."
— D. H. Lawrence, *"Snake"*

When I open your letter, your anger flashes out
at my page, missing from your *schrift*. I'd met
you once: at a reading and soirée to fête
your one hard-won, hard-bound book. So what
did my congratulations that day miss? *"You missed*
your chance. My real friends thanked me, with signed
books, checks, poems of praise. But you? The list
of takers who aren't givers gets around.

"You'll pay for your ingratitude," you say,
shifting the cost of my naïveté.
Now I know how Lawrence would have felt
before that water trough at Etna's foot
had the snake turned, hissed *"Coward"* at him,
then whiplashed back into its darkened realm.

Carolyne Wright

ONE MORNING

> *" . . . the split second between summer's*
> *Sprawling past and winter's hard revision . . ."*
> — Edward Hirsch, "Fall"

Dreaming under my quilt in the owl-gray dawn
Of these high ranges, I feel sunlight home in,
Making the quilt's red diamond patterns shine.

Rainbows of reflected light nestle at the border
Of my comforter as shadows of late summer
Slip through the windows and screen door,

Flickers' wings flash through the aspen
And dry lightning electrifies the canyon.
I throw aside my sleep and step into the garden.

Let winter come—summer's passing sprawl
Gives itself up to flocks that assemble their V-shaped call,
Relinquishing the beautiful ache of approaching fall.

SONETO DESESPERADO

"Puedo escribir los versos más tristes esta noche." — Pablo Neruda

How, love, can I speak to you my saddest lines
from this long pier in solitude before dawn,
recalling you, my captain of abandon
stunned between sea walls in the shipwrecked lanes?
Could I flash semaphore's wisdom toward your pearl-rimed eyes,
eyes that failed as twilight's signal flares plundered
the storm's ravages? Your doomed schooner foundered,
waves splintered the hull in plummeting skies.

How can I ask? You have no answers for me,
lost voyager in your ferocious berth
submerged like an amphora in the dark
while I cling to desire like an ark
that navigates dead oceans of a darkened earth,
woman between shipwreck and a moonless sea.

Carolyne Wright

EULENE WITH ROBINSON
ON THE GOLDEN GATE BRIDGE
— 18 July 1955

Robinson, don't jump. The water's too dark
Here, the current under the towering iconic
Spans too swift, the view of the Pacific
Too wild a surmise for the circling shark.

Come, let's stroll back to your Plymouth, retrieve
The keys, and let me drive you home. Where
Do you live, Robinson? Where does your despair
Drop like a dying fern? Get in, sit down, and leave

The rest to me. From your Savoy's passenger seat
Enjoy the passing show. Here is the Presidio's
Greensward, and there's Nob Hill—and Royal Cortissoz?
Ghosting the Tenderloin, an easy mark on Market Street.

Over there is North Beach, and City Lights, soon to beam
Its heady glow . . . and now we're cruising thru the Haight—
You don't want to miss the Sixties, Mr. R., straight
Though you lace yourself. Wondrous life, eh? A dream

From which you'd have to waken if you drowned.
Here's your pad, R. Whaddya say? I'll wait here
Curb-side, while you collect your red socks, your *noir*
Fedora; give mewling Lonesome a bowl of cream
And the flat's keys to the super. Let's split this scene,

R. Don yr shades, kick back, turn up the radio
And check out the redwoods, Big Sur, Monterrey,
The coast! The open road! Two days, we'll hit L.A.,
Groovin' all the way to the border *¡Ay, Jalisco!*
Señor Robinson, we're Mexicali-bound!

LEGS THIN AS BRANCHES

The muse when it is new
wobbles on legs thin as branches.
It bleats and mewls,

not a horse to be ridden,
only another baby
needing milk and love.

You have to believe in what isn't there
a long time before it begins
to be there. Years pass

before you dare put a saddle
on its back, before you dare
climb up and weigh the reins

in your hands. When it is new
the muse stirs you
to practice faith in the music

of what you cannot hear,
to make art of what you cannot see.
When the day dawns

for you to trust your weight to it,
sit up straight. Gather all
that its long becoming

has brought forth in you.
Look steadily in the direction
you must go.

ENGLISH CAFÉ

She greets us with a simile,
the daily specials listed on her oversized thesis.
Will you have regular or irregular verbs?

My friend orders braised clause
with a side of apostrophes. I choose
small plates of articles and prepositions.

But no dative? the waitress asks,
No genitive? She offers Shakespeare
or D. H. Lawrence for dessert.

We sip from snifters of Strunk & White,
share adverbs while coordinating
conjunctions rise languidly

to dance. Between parentheses,
a gerund cracks jokes. We pay
in participles, tip a metaphor.

You've forgotten your predicate,
the waitress calls after us, dangling
a modifier on a ring of rhymed nouns.

WHERE IT MIGHT LEAD YOU

Words stir in the basement room,
the laptop drowsing off to sleep

amid snapshots and Christmas wrap.
She sits cross-legged on the bed

in her nest of poems and pens and books
lying open. She might be Ariadne,

finding her way through the labyrinth,
following her red thread

to whatever the day will hold—
lacing up her Nikes and setting out

through sleeping streets, crow
calling from the laurel, a calico

cat on the hood of a car.
The muddle of daughters waking,

upstairs, their cartoons, *Scooby
Doo*, the newspaper, *Dear Abby*,

spilled Cheerios. She reels in the skein
of the morning and holds it,

just for a moment,
like a cold star.

Bethany Reid

WHEN POEMS SIT VACANT

"When poems sit vacant for a long time, they can attract squatters."
— real estate story which I misheard on KUOW-FM, NPR's Seattle affiliate

An old poem will suit best, maybe Aphra Behn
or a lyric by Sappho, something with the doors
falling askew from their hinges. A poem only a few
decades forgotten will do. Avoid the ones

too often anthologized, with the herds
of college freshmen tramping through.
Find a capacious poem, if not in lines then in depth,
a poem with secret crannies. Windows,

even broken, will let in the light. I can recommend
an obscure sonnet by Gerard Manley Hopkins,
quiet as a monastery, or a verse by Edna
St. Vincent Millay with long porches and shade.

Pull a rocking chair out to that porch.
If the sun isn't shining, no matter. Being alone
in the lines will be enough. Smell the rain.
Listen to the thunder of the sweet, old rhymes.

CROSSROADS

In this spirit, stone speaks
In this stone, imagination flies
In this breath, truth lives
In this life, spirit sings
In this song, birds dance
In this dance, we begin

SEARCHING FOR MATTHEW
— for Susan

Today searchers comb Pratt Creek
in the heart of the Cascades. They
are looking for one small boy, aged
thirteen, who had been lagging behind
the others. Or so the Scout Master
says. His words and our hopes, like
the seventy-two-mile area, are dampened
by occasional drizzle and blanketed
with clouds.

The thirty-five searchers examine
hiking trails, cliffs, steep embark-
ments, heavy brush and their own sad
spirits. Yes, they would rather be indoors
at this late hour, feet perched on a wood
stove's curved fender, hands warming
iced cans of beer. They ask themselves:
has he fallen. Does he sleep. Does he
dream. Have they overlooked him. Can they
fail. Will it snow. Will the mountain
claim him. No, they persuade themselves.

Small boys do love games. What if he
waits just ahead, watching. Watching.
They try calling the boy out from
his hiding place. Matthew. Matthew.
But only the mapped places answer.
Their magical names stir
in the near freezing dark: Olallie, Kaleetan,
Tuskahatchie, Snoqualmie, Guye,
and the legend deep in the heart of it all
Granite Mountain itself.

Beneath this data, this information,
these facts, are the questions that plague
us. Indeed, Why is he lost. Whom does
he follow. And should we have given
him more than those four plastic jars
of trail mix, a sleeping bag and a change
of dry clothing. And what do mothers
say of their children, their sons
who, perhaps, are always small boys
searching for those owl-eyed trolls, at
some trail's end, that await them and
beckon them into the forest.

We see, or think we see, where our
children have gone. Yet, it is they
alone, our Matthews, who know where
they are and where they are going.
Like this fierce wind pushing itself free
from the cold mists and mosses shrouding
Granite Mountain, they are not lost.
They know the terrain. We must believe
they will find this creek where the
searchers are gathered, and in tracking
its ancient source, our children will
somehow make their own peace
with the dark.

GREETINGS!

Somewhere is east of here
a solid city not hard to spot

Nowhere is private
an empty town at
the edge of my eye
a meandering street
with vacant lots

Sixty-five townsfolk
who look like me
sun themselves on
sixty-five porches
that look like this one

All in all
a good place to visit
nice to write from

No postage for nightmares
and snapshots fold easy

ARS POETICA:
SCAR TISSUE

Blood is a place
where pain doesn't live

Memory is a house
that doesn't like pain

My house has no door
it lets in the wind

Enter quietly and
sit in the parlor

I bruise easily

ODE TO MY HEADACHE

Persistent, unwilling
To yield
    to two ibuprofen
    to caffeine
    to a nap.
You, strong and powerful gladiator,
    have vanquished them all.
You have taken refuge
    in my left temple
    in my left cheekbone
    above my left eye.
Like a John Wayne or Clint Eastwood,
you will defend what is yours.
While I wish
I could just
convince you
to ride off
into the sunset.

SHATTERED

You must hold the egg of grief gently
or the white will run clear
through your fingers, fall
to the floor, mix
with slivers of shell, leave
a slick, sharp mess at your feet

while in your palm you hold the broken

yolk

that used to be the sun.

THE GARDEN

Want to woo your lady fair?
Show her your secret garden where
you will find flowers of every hue,
the softest of yarrows, pinks and blues,

carnations, fox glove, poppies so red,
tulips and roses to pillow her head.
Mock orange and the hollyhock
will turn her into a forget-me-not.

Nasturtium, forsythia and lupine
amidst their fragrances she'll recline.
Petunia, pansy and herbal rue,
her love forever will stay true.

Among the tulips and daffodil,
this fantasy you can now fulfill,
but you must not hesitate:
floral sheets on sale $10.98!

TATTOO
(In a man's voice)

When I was in the Navy
I got liquored up one night,
stumbled into a tattoo parlor
to get myself beautified.

I've an eagle on my shoulder
and a snake climbing up my spine,
but you ain't seen nothin'
'til you've seen that wife of mine.

She's a daisy on her ankle
and a rose behind her ear
and a peacock on her shoulder
that goes from here to there.

She has a doughboy on her bottom
and a mandala on her knee,
a sailboat on her stomach
that rocks like she's out to sea.

She has some crazy design on her elbow
and a bow at the top of her crack,
a heart on her left breast
and angel wings on her back.

Now, I love this lady very much
I'd hate for us to part.
So when she dies, I'll skin her hide
and hang it up for art.

MOUNT RAINIER

"O beautiful for spacious skies,
For amber waves of grain,
For purple mountain majesties
Above the fruited plain . . ."

Why can't I write
words like that
which flow sweetly
from my lips,
instead of words
that rhyme and chime
and from my mouth da—rips.

As I gaze
across the plains
at lovely Mount Rainier
the only words
I muster up are from
a commercial for cold beer.

HOREHOUND CANDY

Seeing it on the country store shelf
reminds me of Dad.
"Horehound Candy," a name snickered
at when I got older,
a flavor not really to my liking,
a root beer licorice cough drop taste,
but still, it was candy
and what kid would turn down candy.

Dad would always buy one stick,
snap it in two, hand me my half,
say "too much sugar'll spoil supper,
plus a penny a piece is ridiculous."

I don't remember the first or last
time he bought me a stick;
I just remember he always did,
a sort of father-son rite of passage
when horehound was on the shelf.

So I ask for one of the candies,
pay the ridiculous price of a quarter
and put half the stick in my mouth.
It tastes just like it did back then,
but I don't remember when it ever
caused tears to fall from my eyes.

I received a cookie cutter form letter of rejection from the editor for someone else's poem in my SASE. That someone else sent me the acceptance letter she received for my poem in her SASE.

My poetic response: this seventeen-syllable "precursory curse" villanelle.

Dear Editor,

I appreciate the time you took to send this rejection letter
about your decision not to publish me or put my work in print,
but I think, indeed, you really need to do your rejections better.

With your fine job title I felt you'd be the writing standard setter
'til you rejected me in an SASE someone else had sent.
Should I appreciate the time you took on this rejection letter?

My intent is not to anger or put my future chance in fetter,
nor is the matter of this patter solely to chastise you or vent,
but I think, indeed, you really need to write your rejections better.

Some of my best saved rejections have never fed a paper shredder;
that's how I detect, in retrospect, rhyme and reason to circumvent
the monumental task you took to construct this rejection letter.

Try to get the right writer's name in your rejection letter header
or you may wonder where the submissions for your next edition went.
So I think, indeed, you really need to write your rejections better.

In closing, I'll just make this point I surely hope you will consider:
Always remember you cannot edit what we writers never sent.
Though I appreciate the time you took on your rejection letter,
still I think, indeed, you really need to check your rejections better.

Yours Truly,
Carl "Papa" Palmer ~ writer

FOUND SONNETS

Walking my dog one cold rainy night,
my two feet behind four paws ahead of mine,
we walked the parking lot without fright
or hesitation, knowing we were fine;

suddenly the dog stopped to find
muddied polyester fiber-filled headless
plush toys someone left behind:
dog, bear, rabbit, dolls abandoned, neat no less—

clothes strewn, toothbrush, hair brush all on the ground,
schoolbooks, notebooks, paperbacks' wet
discarded stories, fiction unfound.

I picked up a book, left others with much regret:
garbage to some, but *Shakespeare's Sonnets*?
Still dry for me to enjoy all the canzonets!

MONK'S DREAM ON MONET'S *NYMPHÉAS BLEUS*

In a dream splashed
with purple notes
tenor sax lilies float
a masterpiece in blue.

Monk strikes high octave
light changes soft tone
snare drums turn lilies
color, soft shadows

behind the double bass
purple pond dream in blue
Monk's *Bleus,*
Monet's world.

ONLY A DREAM

Last night you entered my dream
with the sound of violins and cellos
very slowly like Aaron Copland's
"Appalachian Spring"

Then you, yes, you changed the tone
cracked the dream open
the way Beethoven played piano
in "Emperor" Rondo: Allegro

I floated with you above the ceiling high
cracked the ceiling through
dissipated in the cold air of night
to find myself wet, after the rain

woken up by the pink tongue
of the dog on my lips
reminding me I have to go to work
under the rain and the sweet floating dream of you.

THE HACKERFOCKY

with apologies to Lewis Carroll

'Twas google and the oldsy yahoo
    Did yawn and twitter on the net
All vixens were the babyboos
    And our lilt crocks confet

Beware the Hackerfock, my son,
    With pics that lie, posts that kill
Beware the cyber bull, Facebook shun
    The criminy slackerwill

He took his fermal mouse in hand
    Long search for nerdist foe he scoured
Distracted he by eBay ads
    YouTube cats devoured

And, in his unprotected viewing,
    The Hackerfock with tools of shame
Attacked with virus spewing
    And IM'd as it came

The fermal mouse went clickity click
    Zero, one, Zero, one, track and track
He quarantined and took its head
    Message-boarding frack

And hast thy newbie slain Hackerfock?
    Emoticons to you, dear boy,
Oh yangpo day! Vacroo! Bishay!
    They gleetexted in their joy

'Twas google and the oldsy yahoo
    Did yawn and twitter on the net
All vixens were the babyboos
    And our lilt crocks confet

IDIOTISMS

Wiser and older
he avoids long walks
and all piers.

He noticed
no silver
when he cut open
the cloud.

The new president quickly
signed the amendment
making Tomorrow
eighth day of the week.

THE NEXT LIFE

Is death a beginning,
or is it an ending?

Should we be saving
or spending?

KNOWLEDGE

An edge is a border: a clipped, geometric
hedge. A threshold: the kind you cross
when you make a pledge. An edge like a shelf
is a ledge. When two edges join at sharp angles,
they make a wedge. Add a third edge, and that's
a triangle: the shape of the stem of a sedge.
Birds have an edge over cats, but not till they fledge.
There's a village in Suffolk called Nedging,
but no one there knows what it means to nedge.
Sharp edges help when you ski or sledge,
but the best edge of all is knowledge: knowing
that when you're becalmed you can always kedge,
or that if you're in Gothenburg, Sweden, on Walpurgis Night
you're just in time for the Chalmers Cortège.
Or you could just veg.

MY DARLING CLEMENTINE

Corybantic apodictic
Flummadiddle mangosteen
Fuscous giglet bosky chaffer
Hebetudinous shebeen

Fubsy drumlin dinkum crasis
Dasypygal wifty bort
Pawky fartlek clepe cadastral
Papuliferous dehort

Yabber spurtle grig schmegeggy
Snollygoster astrobleme
Mingy boodle skookum quidnunc
Circumbendibus bedeen

Scut caruncle furphy fizgig
Valetudinarian
Mackle eke pyx ween embrangle
Borborygmus gegenschein

13 CONSTRAINTS, 14 ACKNOWLEDGMENTS, AND 11 PLEDGES

I will never decide to kill from miles away and miles above.

I will never be raped or beaten by someone I tried to love.

I will never love everyone all at once.

I will never zip into stars-and-stripes leather and undertake desperately reckless stunts.

I won't be arrested because of my race.

I won't be exalted because of my face.

I will never receive a giant blue ribbon for my exemplary meat pets.

I will never triumph in straight sets.

I won't be described in print as a kingpin.

I won't ever make the most of LinkedIn.

I will never die in my prime.

I will never portray the human condition through mime.

I will never run off to a nunnery, my breasts in a sack and a band on my finger to show I'm married to someone who won't ever leave me or lie, or, if he does, it won't be his fault.

I will never shoot because you didn't halt.

I will never be a popular girl.

I will never vote for a psychotic churl.

I won't ever rise before dawn and tend to the cows.

I'll never smear ashes on congregants' brows.

I won't visit 1% of the places I've seen in pictures.

I won't show up often enough to be remembered as one
of the fixtures.

I will never cling to a coconut palm while my family and
all my possessions are swept out to sea.

I will never enjoy my pick of women, nor they theirs of me.

I will never possess the most comprehensive collection.

I will never reveal my perverse predilection.

I will never grow up in Scotland, saying *bothy* and *sklent*,
telling the boys *Ca' canny, lads!*

I will never again wear prints with plaids.

I won't go commando. Not at my age.

I won't request a lower wage.

I won't ever grasp string theory, though I might try to make
  inappropriate use of all those squiggled-up hidden dimensions.

I won't ever learn Greek or Latin declensions.

I will never whip slaves and then get them pregnant.

I will never get used to the texture of eggplant.

I will never be known to my close friends as "Spanky."

I will never, never ever, root for the Yankees.

I won't ever flee the land of my birth to a country where
  nobody understands.

I won't ever front a succession of locally popular bands.

I will never spread myself over the earth as an omnipresent vapor.

I will never entirely get it onto the paper.

OH, THE HUMANITY!

I have waited all my life for the return of Zeppelins,
those city-block-long airships that bombed London
and burst into tinted flames in Howard Hughes's first movie,
Hell's Angels. A warren of cells of steel girders
dense with hydrogen, the dragon's breath waiting to ignite.
I long for passing dirigibles to dapple me in shadows,
to feel immersed in slow intervals of impossible suspension.
Offspring of the Teutonic count, Zeppelins
were lighter-than-air vessels crafted from steel
and the Prussian will. The needle that supported King Kong
when he leaned out to swat down a biplane
was built to moor the snout of a Zeppelin.
I have waited all my life, probably in vain,
for the return of Count Zeppelin's bombing train in the sky,
carrying gondolas filled with placid passengers
like milk cows conveying full udders across pool table pastures.
I have waited all my life to book a flight in a dirigible
across the pond, rising above all storms and motion sickness,
sipping unspilled champagne while pacing the moon's reflected smirk
in an Atlantic mirror. Like the crippled boy too slow
to follow the other children into the piper's Eden,
I am still waiting.

BUT WHAT IF

It would be so simple
if everything were a conspiracy.
It was the Knights Templar
aimed the planes at the towers.
Every tube of toothpaste
is injected with fluoride
by an Illuminati hand.
The feathering vapor trails
spiderwebbing the sky
all lead back to the Bilderberg Group.
The man behind the curtain
is not kidding:
he really is pulling the levers
releasing the dogs of war,
the piranhas of poverty,
the supercilious cats of corrupt politicians.
It is good to have diagrams,
flow charts, time lines
from which to hang
the dripping wet laundry of paranoia.

PLEASE DON'T PET MY SERVICE ANIMAL

Please don't pet my service animal.
Alligators startle easily.
I'm the only human she abides.
I know what parts of her hide she likes scratched.
Please don't step on my service animal's tail.
She can break your legs if she wants to.
Only my alligator can get me out of the house.
Walking with my alligator reduces my stress.
I have a letter from my doctor and a license from the state.
She still fits on the bus. What's the fuss?
Talking to strangers about my alligator makes me nervous.
My service pet knows when I'm nervous
and she doesn't like it.
I'm going to stand up now.
It's better if you wait until we're off the bus to move.
Alligators tend to lunge at peripheral motion.
Thank you for being quiet.
Both of us like it when people are quiet.
Thank you for helping us relax.

ON THE FIRST DAY OF OCTOBER

The angel of death has no agenda.
The angel of death is not a racist.
The angel of death has no religion.
The angel of death recognizes no borders.
The angel of death is known to every tribe.
The angel of death is beyond politics.
The angel of death cannot distinguish a pound of gold
    from a pound of lead.
The angel of death cannot hear music.
The angel of death has no sense of smell.
The angel of death can neither laugh nor cry.
The angel of death has no understanding of mercy.
The angel of death has no need for understanding.
You cannot make peace with the angel of death by dispensing death.
The angel of death is the shadow we are born with.

THE BRIDGE

It is a bridge to nowhere
its end is not in sight
disappearing in the mist
as dense as is the night

'Tis not a bridge for passage
and few dare go this way
for the unknown is a sign
to keep us all at bay

But great mystery lingers
about what lies beyond
shrouded in drapes of mist
which some great god has drawn

Some have ventured, none returned
and only they can know
what lies at the bridge's end
o'er waters down below

RUSTLING

My house stays open, wind blows through.
It rustles into the house and pulls a scrap
along the hallway, a letter from before

I'd forgotten to read. The curtains sway,
the furniture decays, I live alone.
        My house is open, wind blows through.

In the middle of the living room
are the open eyes of chests I've carried
up the hallway, full of letters from before.

I have only one resolve: I won't shut a lid,
won't hold a single letter from the air.
        Let my house stay open, wind blow through.

Now I sing to the doorjamb, the cat on the sill.
I sing to the night air that leaks through
the hallway, over all the letters from before.

Once I lived in these rooms with you,
once I shut the windows, locked the door.

        Now my house stays open, the wind blows through,
rustling the rooms, the letters all over the floor.

Jo Gale

I am out with lanterns, looking for myself

— *Emily Dickinson*

Lantern flickers dance on shadow lace
and in their back and forth I remember
how my body grew to this place—
a woman by the side of her father
and mother, knowing all that was is now.
It isn't long until the rain blows dark
the flames. So I stand in the garden, low
with the heavy wet, my dress dyed black.

If I find her, what will I say or do—
will she step from the road into the yard?
Will we pack our trunks, at last bid *adieu*?

Or will I lay these lanterns by the hatch,
ascend the stairs to the door—lift the latch—

THE VISIT

In midnight's unfamiliar air I stand,
a stranger to this darkened room, and watch
a meadow fringed with maples, sure that deer
on willow legs, their blood taut with the smell

of March, their dun-gray flanks caught by the moon,
must appear, must leave those deeper shadows,
trio of girls from some Gothic romance
floating in muslin gowns over the grass.

The field is just my friend's Amherst back yard.
Morning, we'll go to see Emily's house.
For now, I wait while clouds rewrite the stars
as light and fleet as memory's last ghosts.

HANDS EMPTY

Behind my eyes the pale ghost I know
hides between the trunks and leaves, a trick
in vision, what I saw—light in the row
I thought I'd follow down the hill, thick
through years away, the windfalls left rotting,
the coop out back forlorn, a few feather
serifs nestled in dirt and all the knotting
questions tight before dark weather.
Here I find
some ruby
fruit to bite
before I
leave, the long
days gone—
and must I
go, give up
my hunger
for these trees,
gnarled canopy
of Winesaps
and Starkings
beneath this
wind sky, must
I start again,
hands empty?
Dear specter, step into the orchard grass
and let me see your face. Or let me rest
inside this green, feel the wind pass
through the sun's prisms. May this harvest
write its answers on the sky's wide glass,
the weighted limbs, the years I loved the best.

IN A SHOE LIVES WHO

And what do you think of that nail-shod shoe,
not the slipper of glass that neatly fit
on Cinderella's soot foot—but that home

for the woman wizened amid her rhyme
of children, her hair gone grey, cheeks as red
as windfall apples waiting for the hands

of children hungry, runny noses, hands
open for the bowl, the spoon. She said *shoo,
eat before the owl's who*. When Mother read

whipped them all soundly, the switch didn't fit
the picture. Perhaps a rumor? The rhyme
of *bread-bed* nesting in my childhood home

with those babes in the woods too far from home,
curled like kittens, their hair, their knees, their hands
covered by leaves the small birds brought, the rhyme

of sorrow, no rhyme of *death*, *breath*, a shoo-
in for the most tragic story to fit
inside that big book when I learned to read,

but here is a whole herd of children, red
as roses, and the woman smiles, at home
with a house built on a sole, windows fit

in the uppers, the orchard's creaking hands
and now the real kids packed into the shoe
sleep a real sleep as the circling stars rhyme

to the hey-diddle over the moon, the rhyme
of sheep, Little Jumping Joan, Robin Red
Breast, Peter's pumpkin, woman in her shoe,

the woman with a bare cupboard at home,
no bone for the dog. We open our hands
to the stories, try to make the rhymes fit

into our days. Maybe she threw a fit
with all that running around her, the rhyme
wearing her down at the day's end, her hands

deep into the dishes, her hands chapped red
and yet in the morning she wakes at home,
steps out the door at the heel of the shoe

fitting into dawn her whole life at home
in the shoe, the sun a red bonnet, hands
a rhyme nesting, and we could live there too.

HOURS OF SEPTEMBER

Here in this blue,
this aging sunlight, the trees
shed a harvest, a psalm

unwinding the woods,
our small salvations snagged
in the branches, in the grass.

Unfolding, we have looked
long at our maps, traced
state routes with no way

back to hear the dead.
That psalm draws its coat
around our shoulders,

and under the great bear,
under the star for north
and the stars we cannot see

over our gardens,
over the snails and worms,
the creek down the road,

winter a dog scratching
at the back door,
night in his throat.

AT THE BRONX-WHITESTONE BRIDGE

I nearly hear the angels sing,
        the north tower ahead like a monument,
                the sun descending its marble staircase
through the day's rose-hinged clerestory—

after bluffing 700 miles,
        a gamble of numbered routes,
                directions checked every exit, trying
to reach LaGuardia, please, before dark—

I slow toward the tollbooth,
        the road a field of cars
                and in my throat a prayer of thanks
for safe passage through Connecticut.

My hands loosen the wheel just once
        before I pay to cross into Queens
                as dusk hangs in the air,
the city's grit turned celestial.

Chords thrum in my chest,
        harp strings plucked so close to where
                I'm going—and barely past the middle
of my life I haven't started,

each bridge the next departure,
        each rising moon the new card dealt,
                all the clouds like wings,
all the drivers kind.

ACKNOWLEDGMENTS

The editor gratefully acknowledges prior publications of poems appearing in this book:

PATRICIA BOLLIN:
"Framework": *Mezzo Cammin*

DENNIS CASWELL:
"My Darling Clementine": *Light.com*

WENDY CHIN-TANNER:
"Before the Fall": *Moonsick Magazine*
"How the Sea": *Horse Less Review*
"On the Oregon Coast in Fall": *Mead*

RICK CLARK:
"camped up river" and "father and son": *Living Senryu Anthology* (online)
"father and son": *Wrenzai Insight Journal* (online)
"the one-legged sparrow" and "a small bird chirps": *Bug-eyed & Bird-brained: Small Creature Haiku* (Red Moon Press, 2016)
"the one-legged sparrow": *Every Cow, Chicken, Fish and Frog: Animal Rights Haiku* (Middle Island Press, edited by Robert Epstein and Miriam Wald, 2016)
"the one-legged sparrow": 2014 Grand Prize Winner, 6th Yamadera Basho Memorial Museum English Haiku Contest

DOUGLAS COLE:
"Morgan Street Junction Café, 4 pm on Monday": *The Gold Tooth in the Crooked Smile of God* (Unsolicited Press, 2018)

MARY ELIZA CRANE:
"Dawn at the Bay of Pigs": *Pudding Magazine: The Journal of Applied Poetry*
"Living Alone": *The Raven Chronicles*

KAREN FINNEYFROCK:
"The Crush": *CityArts Magazine*
"The Crush": *Courage: Daring Poems for Gutsy Girls*, edited by Karen Finneyfrock, Mindy Nettifee, and Rachel McKibbens (Write Bloody Publishing, 2014)

JOSEPH GREEN:
"Come Again?" and "The Philosophy of the Motel Pool": from *What Water Does at a Time Like This* (MoonPath Press, 2015)
"Come Again?": *Terrain.org: A Journal of the Built + Natural Environments*
"The Philosophy of the Motel Pool": *Kudzu: A Digital Quarterly*, *LitSpeak Dresden*, and *Pontoon*

SHARON HASHIMOTO:
"The Bus Driver's Wife": *North American Review*
"The Outer Limits": *Many Mountains Moving*
"Those Left to Tell: For A.C.": *The Same*

CHRISTOPHER J. JARMICK:
"The Hackerfocky": from *Not Aloud* (MoonPath Press, 2015)

RICHARD KENNEY:
"Day Moon" and "Slow Blue": *Poetry Northwest*
"Easter Wings": *Narrative*
"Necessity": *The Sewanee Review*

DONALD KENTOP:
"Lunching with Lenin": from *Poets Unite! The LiTFUSE @ 10 Anthology* (Cave Moon Press, 2016)

JIM LUTZ:
"A Bed of Roses," "Empathy," "Point Barrow," and "The Four Seasons": from *Reassembled Dreams* (Lulu.com, 2009). "The Four Seasons" in *Reassembled Dreams* was "The Four Seasons #1."

DAVID MASON:
"Bildungsroman," "Descend," "Hangman," "Security Light," "The Soul Fox," and "To Hygeia": from *The Sound: New & Selected Poems* (Red Hen Press, 2018)
"Bildungsroman": *The Hudson Review*
"Hangman": *Times Literary Supplement*
"Security Light": *The San Diego Reader*
"The Soul Fox" and "To Hygeia": *Virginia Quarterly Review*

COLLEEN J. McELROY:
"Aubade" from *Here I Throw Down My Heart*, by Colleen J. McElroy, © 2012. Reprinted by permission of the University of Pittsburgh Press.
"In Praise of Older Women," from *Sleeping with the Moon*. Copyright 2007 © by Colleen J. McElroy. Used with permission of the University of Illinois Press.
"Webs and Weeds," from *Music from Home: Selected Poems by Colleen J. McElroy* (Southern Illinois University Press, 1976). Reprinted by permission of the author.

KRISTEN McHENRY:
"Slipping," "Why I Didn't Write a Poem Today," and "Persian Flaw": on Kristen's blog, "The Good Typist," thegoodtypist.blogspot.com

ROBERT McNAMARA:
"Venetian Villanelle": *Image*

JED MYERS:
"Family Gathering," "Nomad's House," and "The Wire Said": from *Dark's Channels*, winner of the 2018 *Iron Horse Literary Review* Chapbook Award
"Family Gathering": *Terrain.org: A Journal of the Built + Natural Environments*
"Nomad's House": a "Commended Poem" for the 2017 McLellan Poetry Competition
"The Wire Said": *Portside*
"The Wire Said": winner of the 2016 McLellan Poetry Prize
"The Wire Said": "Laureate's Choice" of the 2016 Maria W. Faust Sonnet Contest

CARL "PAPA" PALMER:
"Dear Editor": *Foliate Oak Literary Magazine*

PAULANN PETERSEN:
"Capital" and "The Ghee-Eater": from *Understory* (Lost Horse Press, 2013). "The Ghee-Eater" in *Understory* was "As for the Appeal of a Certain Avatar's Sweet, Androgynous Looks." "A Municipal Servant Serenades at the Pier" and "On the Aegean": from *Kindle* (Mountains and Rivers Press, 2008)

DEREK SHEFFIELD:
"April" and "Aubade": *Talking River*
"Emergency" and "The Skookum Indian": *Shenandoah*

KEN SHIOVITZ:
"Marco Polo Returns": from *Rules of the Universe* (Rules of the Universe, 2016)

MICHAEL SPENCE:
"A Good Thing": *The Hopkins Review*
"Birch": *Shenandoah*
"Brine" and "The Middle": *The Sewanee Review*
"The Fourth Box": *Tar River Poetry*
"Undertow": *Poetry Daily* and *The New Criterion*

JT STEWART:
"Crossroads": from "Raven Brings Light to This House of Stories" project, part of broadside series "Praise Songs for the House of Light," poems by JT Stewart printed by Mare Blocker. Part of permanent installation in the Allen Library lobby and on the Second Floor Bridge, between Allen North and Allen South, University of Washington, Seattle. Project sponsored by the Washington State Arts Commission and the Art in Public Places program, in partnership with the University of Washington. Visit www.lib.washington.edu/suzzallo/visio/raven.

JEAN SYED:
"A Valentine for Darby": from *Sonnets* (Dos Madres Press, 2009)
"A Valentine for Darby": *St. Anthony's Messenger*
"Comfort Cat": *Bonney Lake Writers Senior Center Newsletter*

DAVID THORNBRUGH:
"Please Don't Pet My Service Animal": *Capitol Hill Times*

RICHARD WAKEFIELD:
"By Winter Light": *Measure*

CAROLYNE WRIGHT:
"Eulene with Robinson on the Golden Gate Bridge": from *Aspects of Robinson: Homage to Weldon Kees* (The Backwaters Press, edited by Christopher Buckley and Christopher Howell, 2011)
"One Morning": The poem "One Morning" by Carolyne Wright first appeared in Bright Hill Press's *Like Light: 25 Years of Poetry and Prose by Bright Hill Press Writers*, published in 2017. Bright Hill Press has granted permission for the poem to be reprinted in *Footbridge Above the Falls*.

ABOUT THE CONTRIBUTORS AND EDITOR

Lana Hechtman Ayers, night-owl, coffee-enthusiast, star-gazer, has authored nine poetry collections and a romantic time-travel novel, *Time Flash: Another Me*. She manages several poetry presses and works as a manuscript consultant. Lana resides on the Oregon coast, where she enjoys the perpetual plink of rain on the roof and the sea's steady whoosh. Visit her online at LanaAyers.com.

James Bertolino taught creative writing for thirty-six years and retired from Willamette University in Oregon, where he was Writer-in-Residence. His twelfth volume of poetry is *Ravenous Bliss: New & Selected Love Poems* (MoonPath Press, 2014). His national awards include the Discovery Award and a National Endowment for the Arts Fellowship. He served as editor for the anthology *Last Call*, just published by World Enough Writers.

Robinson Bolkum allegedly hails from the iron sulfide catacombs of Jupiter's largest satellite, Ganymede. Bolkum (affectionately known to South Wales gentry as Fenwyck Hieronymus III) arrived on our cozy 3-bedroom planet via low-impact asteroid (nonstop) to Madrid. There, he was raised by gypsies, wolves, rough-housing Swedes, & a trash-talking parrot. With son & wife, an' two of her adult grand-kids, he lives in Marysville, Washington.

Patricia Bollin was raised in Chicago but has lived in Portland, Oregon, since 1973. She serves as Board President of Soapstone, a non-profit dedicated to supporting women's writing. She worked as program officer for the national service program AmeriCorps in Oregon. Her poetry has appeared in print and online publications, including *The Fourth River*, *Clackamas Literary Review*, *Tulane Review*, and *Mezzo Cammin*.

Anita K. Boyle is a poet and an artist who is a lifetime resident of Northwest Washington. Her books include *What the Alder Told Me*, *The Drenched* and *Bamboo Equals Loon*, and another book is forthcoming from MoonPath Press. She lives in Bellingham, where she writes collaborative poetry with her husband-partner-friend James Bertolino.

John Byrne lives in Albany, Oregon, with Cheryl French, an artist, and their daughter Sean: a writer, actor, and college student. He writes formal poems, plays, and short stories. His poems have appeared in many journals, and his plays have been performed in small theaters in over ten states around the country. His poems often celebrate the delights of getting older with a wonderful partner.

Dennis Caswell is the author of the poetry collection *Phlogiston* (Floating Bridge Press). His work has appeared in *Bluestem, Crab Creek Review, Poetry Northwest, Rattle,* and assorted other journals and anthologies. He lives outside Woodinville, Washington, and works as a software engineer in the aviation industry. He hopes to retire someday soon, so he can devote more time to not writing.

Wendy Chin-Tanner is the author of the poetry collections *Turn* (Sibling Rivalry Press, 2014), which was an Oregon Book Awards finalist, and *Anyone Will Tell You* (SRP, 2019). She is a founding editor at *Kin Poetry Journal* and poetry editor at *The Nervous Breakdown.* A trained sociologist, Wendy was born and raised in New York City and educated at Cambridge University, United Kingdom.

Rick Clark is a Seattle poet, editor, and educator. In 2016, Red Moon Press published his book *Bug-eyed & Bird-brained: Small Creature Haiku.* He's also author of *Journey to the River: India Travels* (Pina Publishing, 2016). Recently, Rick placed second in the European Kukai (haiku ranking) and in 2014 won Grand Prize in the 6th Yamadera Memorial Basho Museum English Haiku Contest.

Douglas Cole teaches and lives in Seattle. His latest poetry collection is *The Gold Tooth in the Crooked Smile of God* (Unsolicited Press, 2018). His poetry and fiction have both been nominated for a Pushcart Prize, and his work has appeared in many anthologies and journals, including *Best New Writing, The Raven Chronicles,* and *The Wisconsin Review.* His website is douglastcole.com.

Kevin Craft lives in Seattle and directs the Written Arts program at Everett Community College. His first book, *Solar Prominence* (2005), was selected by Vern Rutsala for the Gorsline Poetry Prize from Cloudbank Books. A second collection, *Vagrants & Accidentals* (2017), was published in the Pacific Northwest Poetry Series of the University of Washington Press.

Mary Eliza Crane resides in the Cascade foothills. A regular feature throughout Puget Sound, she has read poetry from Woodstock to LA. Mary has two volumes of poetry, *What I Can Hold In My Hands* and *At First Light,* published by Gazoobi Tales. Her work has appeared in several journals and anthologies, including *The Raven Chronicles, Pudding, POETS UNiTE,* and *WA 129.*

Clark Crouch, a retired federal executive and independent management consultant, is a poet, publisher, performer, and self-proclaimed Poet Lariat. The editor or author and publisher of twenty books, he capitalizes on his youthful experience as a cowboy in the Sandhills of Nebraska. Two of his poetry books, *Western Images* and *Views from the Saddle,* have won the coveted Will Rogers Gold Medallion for Cowboy Poetry.

Karen Finneyfrock is the author of two young adult novels: *The Sweet Revenge of Celia Door* and *Starbird Murphy and the World Outside*, both published by Viking Children's Books. She is one of the editors of the anthology *Courage: Daring Poems for Gutsy Girls* and the author of *Ceremony for the Choking Ghost*, both released through Write Bloody Publishing.

Victoria Ford graduated from Ohio Wesleyan University and Indiana University. Chapbooks include *Following the Swan* (Fireweed Press) and *Rain Psalm* (Rose Alley Press). Other publication credits include the Poets Against the War website and *Petroglyph*. A former English instructor at Seattle Central College and Antioch University Seattle, she is currently an independent contractor for education companies.

Jo Gale lives and writes in the Pacific Northwest. Her poetry has appeared in *Mezzo Cammin* and *Pilgrimage Magazine*. She received her MFA in Poetry from Seattle Pacific University in 2013 and is currently at work on her first book.

Joseph Green lives in Longview, Washington. His most recent collection of poems is *What Water Does at a Time Like This* (MoonPath Press, 2015).

Sharon Hashimoto has had recent poems appear in *Shenandoah, Enizagam, The Raven Chronicles, North American Review, Blue Lyra Review,* and *Kettle Blue Review.* Her book *The Crane Wife* (Story Line Press, 2003) was co-winner of the Nicholas Roerich Poetry Prize. Recent stories have appeared in *River Styx, Moss,* and *American Fiction.* She is currently at work on a novel.

David D. Horowitz founded and manages Rose Alley Press. His most recent collection is *Cathedral and Highrise* (Rose Alley, 2015). His poems have appeared in many journals and anthologies, including *Candelabrum, The Lyric, The New Formalist, The Raven Chronicles, Terrain.org: A Journal of the Built + Natural Environments,* and *Here, There, and Everywhere,* and his essays regularly appear online in *Exterminating Angel.* His website is www.rosealleypress.com.

Christopher J. Jarmick has curated and hosted monthly poetry readings and events in western Washington since 2001. In 2016 he became the owner of BookTree, an independent new and gently used bookstore in Kirkland, Washington: www.booktreekirkland.com. Chris previously lived in New Jersey, New York, and Los Angeles, where he was a writer/producer for television and film projects and series. His latest poetry collection is *Not Aloud* (MoonPath Press, 2015).

Richard Kenney teaches at the University of Washington and lives with his family on the Olympic Peninsula. His poems in this anthology will take their place in a new book, *Terminator,* scheduled for publication at Knopf in October of 2019.

Donald Kentop has had poems published in numerous anthologies, including several from Rose Alley Press, which also published his first collection, *On Paper Wings*. In 2015 he released *Frozen by Fire: A Documentary in Verse of the Triangle Factory Fire of 1911*.

William Kupinse is Professor of English at the University of Puget Sound. He has been writing about the environmental injustices of fracked gas and its many aliases—"natural" gas, liquid "natural" gas, LNG—since 2006. He stands with the Puyallup Tribe, upon whose traditional lands the city of Tacoma is built, in opposing Puget Sound Energy's illegal LNG refinery.

A 2016 Jack Straw Fellow, an Artist Trust Fellow, and a nominee for a *Stranger* Genius Award, **Robert Lashley** has had poems published in *Feminete*, *The Seattle Review of Books*, NAILED, GRAMMA, *Poetry Northwest* and *The Cascadia Review*. Small Doggies Press published his two full-length poetry collections: *The Homeboy Songs* (2014) and *Up South* (2017).

Priscilla Long is a Seattle-based poet and writer of literary nonfiction, science, history, and fiction. Her five books include a collection of essays titled *Fire and Stone: Where Do We Come From? What Are We? Where Are We Going?* and *Crossing Over: Poems*. She grew up on a farm on the Eastern Shore of Maryland.

Seattle poet **Jim Lutz** was born in 1943 and grew up in St. Louis, Missouri. He divided his college years between newspaper writing and the pursuit of an engineering degree. After graduate school in Australia and Navy service in Antarctica and Barrow, Alaska, he lived in Ketchikan, Alaska, for eighteen years. His collected poems have been published as *Reassembled Dreams* available from Lulu.com.

David Mason's latest books are *Voices, Places: Essays* and *The Sound: New and Selected Poems*. The former poet laureate of Colorado, he currently lives in Tasmania with his wife.

Brendan McBreen is a poet and workshop facilitator with Striped Water Poets. He also writes sci-fi, humor, and haiku, and is a student of Zen and Taoist philosophy, a collage artist, an occasional cartoonist, and an event coordinator with AuburnFest and the Poetry at the Rainbow Café series. Brendan's first book, *Cosmic Egg*, is available from MoonPath Press.

Colleen J. McElroy lives in Seattle, Washington. Her poetry collections include *Queen of the Ebony Isles* (Before Columbus Foundation American Book Award); *Here I Throw Down My Heart* (finalist for the Milt Kessler Book Award, the Walt Whitman Award, the Phyllis Wheatley Award, and the Washington State Governor's Award); and *Blood Memory* (finalist for the 2017 Paterson Poetry Prize).

Kristen McHenry is a poet and fiction writer who lives and works in Seattle. Her work has been seen in publications including *Busk*, *Big Pulp*, *Dark Matter*, and the anthology *Many Trails to the Summit*. She has three published poetry chapbooks as well as a short story chapbook. She is currently seeking publication for her novel, *Day Job Blues*.

Robert McNamara has published three books of poems, most recently *Incomplete Strangers* (Lost Horse, 2013). He has co-translated Bengali poet Sarat Kumar Mukhopadhyay, whom he met on Fulbright to Calcutta, and published their work as *The Cat Under the Stairs* (Eastern Washington University, 2007). A longtime teacher of academic writing at the University of Washington, he retired in 2016 to cultivate his garden.

Jed Myers is author of *Watching the Perseids* (Sacramento Poetry Center) and *The Marriage of Space and Time* (MoonPath Press). Recognitions include *The Southeast Review's* Gearhart Prize, *The Tishman Review's* Millay Prize, and the *Iron Horse Literary Review* Chapbook Award. Poems have appeared in *Rattle*, *Poetry Northwest*, *The American Journal of Poetry*, *Southern Poetry Review*, *The Greensboro Review*, and elsewhere. He's Poetry Editor for *Bracken*.

Ken Osborne has been writing poetry since he was a child. He was born in England, where as a young man he drifted from job to job, eventually becoming a retail executive. He ran the Cambridge Poetry Group, won a few competitions and was published in several magazines. He came to America in 2006 and performs at open mics in and around Redmond, Washington.

Carl "Papa" Palmer of Old Mill Road in Ridgeway, Virginia, now lives in University Place, Washington. He is retired from the military and Federal Aviation Administration (FAA) and is enjoying life as "Papa" to his grand descendants. Carl is also a Franciscan Hospice volunteer and former Pushcart Prize and Micro Award nominee. MOTTO: Long Weekends Forever!

Paulann Petersen, Oregon Poet Laureate Emerita, has published seven full-length books of poetry, including her latest, *One Small Sun* (Salmon Press of Ireland, 2019). The Latvian composer Eriks Esenvalds chose a poem from her book *The Voluptuary* as the lyric for a choral composition that's now part of the repertoire of the Choir at Trinity College, Cambridge.

Bethany Reid's poetry appears in numerous journals, including *Calyx*, *The MacGuffin*, and *Cumberland River Review*. Her book, *Sparrow*, won the 2012 Kenneth and Geraldine Gell Poetry Prize, selected by Dorianne Laux. Her new book, *Body My House*, was released by Goldfish Press in 2018. She lives in Edmonds, Washington, and blogs at www.bethanyareid.com.

Raúl Sánchez is a translator currently working on the Spanish version of his inaugural collection, *All Our Brown-Skinned Angels*, nominated for the 2013 Washington State Book Award in Poetry. He is also a Poetry Mentor for the PONGO Teen Writing Project in the Juvenile Detention Center and a teacher for Seattle Arts and Lectures' Writers in the Schools (WITS) program.

Randolph Douglas Schuder is a longtime Seattle resident, held captive to the diverse Northwest landscapes. Semi-retired, he enjoys many outdoor pursuits, including mushroom foraging, day hiking and backpacking, and, not least, fly-fishing. In 2000, Rose Alley Press published his poetry collection, *To Enter the Stillness*, and later Rose Alley featured his work in two anthologies. He is well-known to the local arts community as a fine art model.

Derek Sheffield's book of poems, *Through the Second Skin*, was a finalist for the Washington State Book Award. His poems have appeared in *Poetry, The Georgia Review, The Gettysburg Review*, and *The Southern Review*, and were given special mention in the 2016 Pushcart Prize anthology. He teaches poetry and ecological writing at Wenatchee Valley College and is the poetry editor of *Terrain.org*.

Ken Shiovitz, PhD, former researcher in animal behavior, is a real estate broker in Seattle. He has hosted poetry venues, acted with a local theatre company and is a member of The Poet's Table Workshop. His publications include studies in bird song, poems, essays and YouTube videos. His recent poetry book is *Rules of the Universe*.

K. Simon earned a PhD in psychology in an area related to human resources. She is the Kirkland Library Writer-in-Residence and President of the Redmond Association of Spoken Word (RASP). When not writing, she enjoys collecting hobbies, such as knitting, acting, and playing Dungeons & Dragons. Her work has appeared in *Sonic Boom Journal, Snakeskin*, and *Poplorish*.

Michael Spence spent thirty years driving public-transit buses in the Seattle area, retiring on Valentine's Day, 2014. His poems have appeared recently or are forthcoming in *The Hudson Review, Measure, The New Criterion, North American Review*, and *Tar River Poetry*. In 2014, he was awarded a Literary Fellowship from Artist Trust. His fifth book, *Umbilical* (St. Augustine's Press, 2016), won The New Criterion Poetry Prize.

Joannie Stangeland is the author of the collections *The Scene You See, In Both Hands*, and *Into the Rumored Spring*, the chapbooks *Weathered Steps* (Rose Alley Press) and *A Steady Longing for Flight*, winner of the Floating Bridge Press Chapbook Award, and the pamphlet *A Piece of Work*. Her poems have appeared in *Prairie Schooner, Mid-American Review, The Southern Review*, and other journals.

JT Stewart (poet / writer / editor / public artist / playwright / teacher) was named the first monthly Poet-in-Residence (February 2017) for *The Seattle Review of Books*. She was Poetry Editor for *A MILLENNIUM REFLECTION: Seattle Poets and Photographers* (University of Washington Press, 1999). Viewers can see her broadsides in the permanent installation *RAVEN BRINGS LIGHT TO THIS HOUSE OF STORIES* in the University of Washington's Allen Library.

Jean Syed is English from Lancashire, went to Birmingham University, and worked in Portsmouth and the East Midlands. She came to Ohio and now lives in Bonney Lake. She belongs to the Ohio Poetry Association and has published in *The Lyric*, *The Raintown Review*, *Calamaro Magazine*, *The Bird Watchers' Digest*, and online in *The Rotary Dial*, *The Journal of Formal Poetry*, and *Lighten Up Online*. Her chapbooks are *Sonnets* (Dos Madres Press) and *My Portfolio* (Kelsay Books).

David Thornbrugh has misspent a lifetime happily spitting watermelon seeds into the vegetable patch of poetry, hoping opium poppies would be the result. In the open mic of his dreams, he sloshes NW microbrews with whomever pressed the Epic of Gilgamesh into clay tablets, Emily Dickinson, William Carlos Williams, and Federico García Lorca. He thanks Rose Alley Press for letting him add to the chaos.

Richard Wakefield has taught humanities at Tacoma Community College for thirty-four years. For over twenty-five years he was a critic for *The Seattle Times*, publishing hundreds of articles, reviews, and essays on contemporary literature. His first poetry collection, *East of Early Winters*, won the Richard Wilbur Award; his second collection, *A Vertical Mile*, was shortlisted for the Poets' Prize.

Connie K Walle is a life-long resident of Tacoma, Washington, where she founded and is President of the Puget Sound Poetry Connection. Through the PSPC, she hosts the Distinguished Writer series, now in its 27th year. MoonPath Press recently published her poetry collection, *What's Left*.

Carolyne Wright's newest book is *This Dream the World: New & Selected Poems* (Lost Horse Press, 2017), whose title poem won a Pushcart Prize and was included in *The Best American Poetry 2009*. Her ground-breaking anthology, *Raising Lilly Ledbetter: Women Poets Occupy the Workspace* (Lost Horse, 2015), received ten Pushcart Prize nominations. A Seattle native, Wright held a 2018 residency at the Instituto Sacatar in Bahia, Brazil.

Other Rose Alley Press Titles

Caruso for the Children, & Other Poems by William Dunlop, 978-0-9651210-2-6, paper, $9.95
"Dunlop is a brilliant metrical technician....richly allusive, a gifted parodist, and often very funny."
—Jonathan Raban

Rain Psalm, poems by Victoria Ford, 978-0-9651210-0-2, paper, $5.95
"Victoria Ford's poems are at once modest and courageous, cut clean and sure..." —Sam Hamill

Cathedral and Highrise, poems by David D. Horowitz, 978-0-9906812-0-5, paper, $9.95
"Horowitz has a gift for rhyming iambic lines." —Rick Clark

From Notebook to Bookshelf: Writing, Publishing, & Marketing
by David D. Horowitz, 978-0-9906812-1-2, velo, $5.95
"*From Notebook to Bookshelf* is a great resource for my students." —Holly Hughes

Resin from the Rain, poems by David D. Horowitz, 978-0-9651210-8-8, paper, $9.95
"These poems display Horowitz's formal clarity and keen ear." —Derek Sheffield

Sky Above the Temple, poems by David D. Horowitz, 978-0-9745024-9-6, paper, $9.95
"*Sky Above the Temple* is a feisty, fervent book." —Martha Silano

Stars Beyond the Battlesmoke, poems by David D. Horowitz, 978-0-9745024-7-2, paper, $9.95
"...a book filled with memorable lines, keen observations, and acute wit."—Lana Hechtman Ayers

Streetlamp, Treetop, Star, poems by David D. Horowitz, 978-0-9651210-5-7, paper, $9.95
"...excellent new book—authentic 'words to cleanse even the sharpest wounds.'"—Carol Robertshaw

Strength & Sympathy: Essays & Epigrams by David D. Horowitz, 978-0-9651210-1-9, paper, $8.95
"...incisive essays and epigrams that take us from proper pronouns to considerate theology."
—Míċeál F. Vaughan

Wildfire, Candleflame, poems by David D. Horowitz, 978-0-9745024-3-4, paper, $9.95
"What a joy it is to read formal verse written by one who has mastered his craft."—Sharon E. Svendsen

Limbs of the Pine, Peaks of the Range: Poems by Twenty-Six Pacific Northwest Poets,
edited by David D. Horowitz, 978-0-9745024-4-1, paper, $12.95
"This anthology offers truth at every turn." —Terry Martin

Many Trails to the Summit: Poems by Forty-Two Pacific Northwest Poets, edited by David D. Horowitz,
978-0-9745024-8-9, paper, $14.95. "What a joy it is to read these poems." —Sharon Cumberland

On Paper Wings, poems by Donald Kentop, 978-0-9745024-0-3, paper, $6.95
"*On Paper Wings* is an accomplished and memorable collection." —Richard Wakefield

To Enter the Stillness, poems by Douglas Schuder, 978-0-9651210-7-1, paper, $6.95
"Douglas Schuder brings uncommonly graceful phrasing to everything he sees." —David Mason

Adam Chooses, poems by Michael Spence, 978-0-9651210-4-0, paper, $9.95
"...elegant design and formal ease we've come to expect of Michael Spence's work."—Madeline DeFrees

Weathered Steps, poems by Joannie Kervran Stangeland, 978-0-9651210-9-5, paper, $6.95
"*Weathered Steps* is a book about all that you almost don't notice, but should." —Melinda Mueller